IMMORTAL HENRY

IMMORTAL HENRY

The Story of a
Lipizzaner Stallion

KENNETH QUICKE

40378

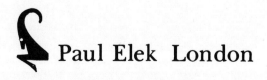 Paul Elek London

First published 1977 in Great Britain by
Elek Books Limited
54–58 Caledonian Road London N1 9RN

Copyright © 1977 Kenneth Quicke

ISBN 0 236 40096 7

Printed in Great Britain by
Unwin Brothers Limited
The Gresham Press, Old Woking, Surrey

Contents

Plates

Between pages 64 and 65

Henry is introduced to Stephen (*photo: F. Knewstub*)
Patricia and Henry on Wimbledon Common (*F. Knewstub*)
Henry, Magic, Stephen and the author (*John of Putney*)
Henry with Magic, Merry, Mystic and Moppet (*F. Knewstub*)
Magic and Merry prepare to pose for Christmas cards
Henry partners Patricia at the Riding School annual Dance (*John of Putney*)
Mystic and Merry pull Cinderella's coach at Wimbledon Theatre (*F. Knewstub*)
Henry performs with his ponies at a gymkhana (*John of Putney*)
Henry and the author perform the Spanish Walk (*John of Putney*)
Henry and the author in medieval attire set out on their first Long Ride to promote the film *Richard III*
Henry and the author arrive at Earl's Court after their second Long Ride (*E.J. Murphy*)
Henry makes an appearance in a children's annual (*IPC Magazines Ltd*)
Henrietta and Henry's spouse and granddaughter (*Sussex Life*)
Immortal Henry (*John of Putney*)

1

The Walk-About

'Have you seen a horse?' I called to a passer-by.

'Many in my time, mate!'

'No — no — I mean a loose one!'

'Oh . . . Is it a white one with a long mane and tail?'

'I hope so!' I answered.

The man thought I was being facetious.

'No — seriously! I've lost one — he escaped from his stable half an hour ago.'

The man grinned. 'Well — I met someone down the road who said he'd seen a horse going into the railway station!'

I realized, knowing Henry, that this was not impossible so I thanked the man and continued on my way. 'Silly fool,' I said to myself, 'you'd think he could answer a simple question.'

My wife had gone off in another direction and I hoped she was getting a better result. Actually there were four of us searching for Henry — the entire staff of our stables.

'Have you lost a horse, then?' yelled a taxi-driver.

'Yes. Have you seen one?'

'A white one with . . .'

'Yes — a long mane and tail! Someone said he was down at the station.'

'The police station?'

'No — the railway station.'

'Ah yes. I saw him going into the goods yard!'

A neighbour drove past and seeing me breathlessly trotting down the road, stopped and offered me a lift. 'Can I drop you somewhere?' he asked.

'Yes — the station goods yard — I think!'

'What on earth are you collecting there?'

'My horse,' I said.

He looked at me quizzically but didn't argue. 'I saw your wife trotting towards the golf club — she was very out of breath —'

'Yes, she's looking for Henry, too.'

'Oh, you've lost him then!'

I had to admit I had. How could Henry embarrass me so much? 'We were doing an advertisement for potato crisps — he had to stand over the wretched man while he ate them from a bag . . .' I explained. I could see my neighbour thought I was mad as he nodded encouragingly.

'That explains everything,' he said.

'It doesn't, you know — Henry was supposed to eat some too, but he suddenly made a funny face and trotted out of the yard!' Traffic was building up and we were caught in a queue. 'This is ridiculous — I think it would be quicker to walk,' I said. 'Do you mind?'

'Pleasure old boy,' he called as I clambered out of the car. 'If I know that stallion of yours he's probably gone off to try fish and chips!'

I darted off towards the station. Trust Henry to choose the rush hour . . .

'What's he doing this time?' called another neighbour from the platform opposite, as I puffed into the station. 'A film on the Iron Horse or a Long Ride to celebrate the coming of the railroad?'

'Seriously,' I said, 'have you seen him?'

Actually he hadn't but of course he had met someone who had. 'Old Mrs Jenkins saw him leaving the greengrocer's with a mouthful of carrots.'

That I quite believed.

'Oh, yes, Henry was here,' said the woman at the greengrocer's. 'He went off towards the cinema. I thought as he was wearing a bridle he must have been with you.' The little woman paused: 'I thought it seemed a bit funny.'

I rushed into the foyer of the cinema opposite and was met by the manageress. 'Don't ask —' she said. 'He's gone round to the car-park. I asked my daughter to take him there. What's he doing — is he on a job?'

'He was,' I gasped breathlessly. 'He didn't care for the subject.'

As I hurried round to the car-park I met the manageress's daughter coming back. 'Is he still there, Yvonne?' I asked.

'No — I forgot the little passageway down to the shops at the back. I think he went down there.'

'Oh damn. Here we go again!'

Down the little passage-way, I dashed.

'What a lovely surprise,' they said at the grocer's, 'Henry coming in for a chat and a tit-bit.'

'I'll give him a tit-bit!' I told them. 'Where is he now for goodness sake?'

'Well, Mrs Bassett at the sweet-shop was saying hullo just now!'

I found no help there either; neither from the sweet-shop, the hardware shop nor the butcher's. He must have been keeping just ahead of me. My quest took me again to the goods yard and I was beginning to suspect that Henry was doing a circular job and was by now wending his way back home!

My neighbour in his car passed me again. 'Have you got him yet?' he called. 'He was coming out of Mrs Smith's house just now!'

I wearily stopped at Mrs Smith's and knocked at the door. 'Have you seen Henry?' I asked.

'Oh yes, bless his heart. He came in for a tit-bit. It reminded me of the days when the milkman had a horse — I always used to give him something.'

'He should have been a milkman's horse — he was made for the job!' I said. 'He might be trained for High School — but he has the mind of a cart-horse!'

'Now you don't mean that! He's such a sweet boy . . . And he seems to know how to look after himself; he left here and went across to Mrs Brown.'

'Oh he did, did he! He must know Mrs Brown dislikes horses!'

'Oh,' said Mrs Smith, 'she doesn't mind Henry. But then, Henry's different, isn't he?'

I nodded. Yes, I supposed that was the truth. Henry was different; he was fearless and he was bold; he was kind and he was honest. Everyone loved him.

'I wonder where the old devil is now?'

Mrs Smith showed some wisdom. 'I shouldn't worry. He's probably home again by now . . .'

How right she was. The clues all led me back to the yard. Henry's walk-about was over and when I got home the television

9

unit was back at work and both he and the little man were munching potato crisps . . .

2

Before We Met

Henry was a Lipizzaner, one of the most rare and beautiful breeds of horses in the world, and he was born on an Alpine stud-farm many years ago. It was really a village because all the houses and buildings had something to do with the stud. There were great white barns in which all the mares and foals lived during the summer months, cobbled stable-yards and freshly painted stallion boxes with the stallions' names in gold lettering over each door. There was an indoor riding school with large airy windows and white-railed paddocks in which the horses were trained. All this — and acres of pastures that went up into the mountains where the herds of Lipizzaners roamed in freedom.

Lipizzaners are known all over the world as the cream of High School, that training above dressage whose movements date back to the days of the fighting man who in battle had to use his horse in such a way to avoid his enemy. The Spanish Riding School in Vienna is still managed as it was centuries ago when the original stock of Andalusian and Spanish horses came to join the school and be taught the 'airs' and the high school movements that we still see there today. The alpine stud at Piber is the most interesting stud in the world; every day the grey mares with their dark foals return through the streets of Piber to their grazing grounds high in the mountains. They say the grazing is in complete harmony, having never had artificial fertilizers, all grasses growing in abundance but never in excess of the others.

Lipizzaners are a smallish breed, seldom more than fifteen hands, have a gentle temperament and submit easily to training. They have a kind and exhilarating personality and large expressive eyes, and partly owing to the centuries of training

11

give you the most balanced ride you could wish for. The breed comes from the original stock of Spanish mares bred at their first stud at Lipizza, and because of this Lipizzaners are still trained and shown at the 'Spanish' School in Vienna. As the original stock were of an even more ancient breed of grey Andalusian, Lipizzaners are usually 'grey' (the horseman's technical term includes white), although browns and blacks have been known. When they perform the ancient musical rides in the white and crystal hall of the Spanish Riding School the Quadrille consists of grey stallions in traditional dress and saddlery. Only the stallions go to Vienna, and not all of those if they prove not up to standard; the mares remain in Piber where some of them at one time were broken to harness and sold as driving horses. Nowadays the stud must pay its way and there are as many bay Anglo-Arabs there as Lipizzaners, all turned out together in the mountains but with uniformed guards on duty all night. If one must keep horses and domesticate them then this is a perfectly wonderful way to do it, perfection in training and in breeding, a breathtakingly beautiful sight to see. Balance and harmony, health and happy obedience — what more could any horseman wish to see?

Henry was named, after his medieval grandparents, Elvolo-toro — but I knew him only as Henry. Like the other foals he was born dark in colour and, like all his breed, became white as he grew older. He was branded on his quarters and this was his first taste of Man, his master. They were long days up in the hills, and he stayed with his dam for nearly a year. He developed a beautiful head with large dark eyes and his mane and tail grew luxuriously long, but his masters decided against him and he was not chosen for final training.

This meant nothing to him. He lived for each day, he grazed in the meadows and he played with others of his own age. In play a Lipizzaner can show aptitude for the movements that are eventually created in his training. Henry floated into that high trot — the passage, he reared into coubette, he balanced himself in levade, he cantered true and he extended into the trot. If only I could have seen him then and known him in the moment of his birth.

I have bred foals and carried them in my arms; a foal is then a helpless youngster without fear, a close contact that will always be a part of some precious thing between you.

I suppose there is always a peak in everyone's life, no matter what the career or job happens to be. Henry was the peak in my career. Even if I did not know it fully at the time, every memory in every passing day tells me now. He was unique.

I was brought up on a farm in the country; my father worked in a city bank and we had a cottage on a 500-acre estate. After the First World War people moved out into the country so the lease on the town house was sold and the farm cottage became our permanent home. The farmer who owned the 500 acres had no son so my two brothers and I were the apples of his eye and we had the full run of the fields and the woods. We worked during the school holidays with the big cart horses, driving them during hay-making and riding them bareback to the meadows in the evening; I suppose this was my first introduction to horses. It soon followed that we had shaggy little ponies in a paddock which we rode every day, we were introduced to hunting, we eventually took advantage of the local Pony Club and our ponies became as much part of the life of the household as were our dogs and our cats and our chickens. This happy state of affairs would have gone on indefinitely, but my father had a car accident which left him a part-invalid and when I, as the youngest son, went off to school the cottage was sold and I never saw it again; sadly I never saw my shaggy pony either. Our life became suburban and during my teenage years, apart from a dog, I knew no other animals and certainly no horses; I missed them very much but never thought about having them back in my life until another tragic thing occurred. In my late teens I developed TB.

Fortunately not for long. But my family immediately thought that a normal life was not to be. After convalescing, what healthy life could I have but one with horses? I could ride, after all, and had some experience with horses. My father had learned to ride in the Army — my Grandma had ridden every morning in Rotten Row — riding was in my blood. Well, perhaps it was but I still had a lot to learn and going into horses wasn't easy.

However, I went to a friend who had horses and taught in her mother's riding school. I had a hard six months before I started taking rides and another six months before I could attempt to take classes. But my mind was made up; horses were indeed a part of my world and I wanted to make them my career. I went through all the phases, show jumping, running a pony trekking holiday centre, having a livery stable, buying and selling horses and going to all the right sales; eventually meeting my wife who was showing hacks and hunters; working as a free-lance instructor, judging classes like local pony events, and finally going into partnership with my wife Patricia in running what became in the early fifties one of the most successful London stables to date.

I was ambitious and increased my business tenfold; we bought a pony farm and bred our own stock, we held open horse shows every month during the summer. Building up a successful business is very much a full-time career, and when it is one that includes animals it can have many pitfalls. We realized this and overcame them — or should I say we weathered them. The teaching side of the business was the only outlet for creation of any kind. We trained our riders to compete and we helped to buy some of them the right horses for the job; but of course everyone who teaches eventually loses his own ability to create. We became so immersed in our training that we gave up our showing. This did not worry Patricia so much as it did me; strangely enough, because she was so brilliant at it, whereas I was mediocre in comparison.

When Henry came into my life I was to have the chance of sublimation . . .

When Henry was born, years before we met, I was staying on a farm in Essex. On the day and at the very hour of his birth I could have been in the fields with my horse or my dog; I could have been with a cow giving birth, or sitting on a tractor with the fresh earth turned and the gulls screaming in my wake. Across those miles from an English farm to an Alpine stud there was forged a link. I may not have been there at his birth but later I was to know him until the day he died. Although I did not know it then he was to give me the best years of his life. They were the best years of my life, too . . .

I shall now try to piece together the events that led to our meeting. Fate had decided we were to meet and, strange as it may sound, I know that I am a better man because of it. It is a privilege to be allowed occasionally to know the mind of an animal, and a horse can accept man as his friend without malice. To have a closeness with any living creature, when thoughts are anticipated, is to know an intimacy and love that cannot be repeated.

Henry was eventually sold to another stud in Portugal. It was a beautiful place with large white-painted boxes and yards shaded with trees. The owner was a famous picador and he trained his stallions to a high degree. Henry stayed there until he matured. He was treated well, exercised on the lunge-rein and sometimes under saddle by experienced grooms. He was now hard and muscular and the picador decided his schooling should commence. Henry showed more aptitude than the Portuguese and the Andalusian stallions and his movement was better than most. Very soon he perfected the passage and the canter changes; he learned to rear and kick out with his hindlegs on command. He used his forelegs to strike and taught himself the high-stepping Spanish Walk; he glided into half-passes and very soon the pirouette. Some said his schooling was too quick because within a year he was ready to show himself off in the bull-ring.

The grand entry was very exciting: the little Lipizzaner pranced in with wide-eyed wonder and his personality was obvious to everyone. At first he was used only for display and the picador chose him because he played to the crowd with such bravado. I like to think he actually did enjoy himself at this time, and knowing now how he enjoyed showing off to a crowd I believe he must have done; the gaiety, the music, the cheering — all this would make him toss his head, use his voice and strike vigorously into his paces. The picador grew to love and respect him but when there were other young stallions coming along to ride, the Lipizzaner sometimes took second place.

Then one day the inevitable happened. They were short of a horse to use in the ring with the bulls and Henry became the obvious choice. Although he was padded and could side-step quicker than most horses, he was unlucky. The bull was clever and turned as quickly as the little stallion; Henry's big eyes were wide with terror as he was caught and thrown onto his side. The bull charged on, the picador scrambled free and Henry was on his feet again in a second — but his near-hind was damaged and there was blood. The crowd roared, someone deflected the raging bull and Henry was rescued from the ring. He was kept at the stud until his leg was sound but of course he carried the scars for the rest of his life. The picador was kind and did not send him in with the bulls again.

15

One day a famous Ambassador came to the bull-ring and was shown an elaborate display which finished with Henry doing the passage and the Spanish Walk. The Lipizzaner behaved beautifully as if he knew this was a special, and last, occasion; the Ambassador was thrilled and enthusiastic about the whole show. At the end of the session, when the fighting was over, the picador rode Henry back into the arena and amid cheering and wild excitement he ceremoniously presented his little stallion as a gift to the Ambassador.

It was a diplomatic gift; perhaps a bit of a white elephant because the Ambassador did not ride well, but he showed his appreciation. His Aide became responsible for Henry's well-being and while they stayed in Portugal a suitable stable was found near the Embassy; members of the Ambassador's staff helped with the exercising and it was a fairly good life. At least they all treated him well and one or two grew possessively fond of him; this feeling for him prevailed throughout his life — there was a mystique — a comaraderie — something indefinable about him which affected everyone who came into contact with him. Even the Ambassador succumbed to his charms and would come to the stables on a number of occasions just to watch him being ridden.

When the Ambassador discovered that his staff could not ride Henry in his advanced movements he was constantly on the look-out for riders with the experience to do so; at Embassy receptions famous riders would accept the invitation to exercise the Lipizzaner. Henry, in consequence, became a firm favourite and was once ridden by one of the riders from the Spanish Riding School in Vienna. This was specially interesting because Henry had left the stud not fully trained. This rider found him surprisingly well-schooled; he said he compared favourably with stallions used at that time in Vienna. His great character must have impressed the rider because years later when he wrote a book he remembered the little stallion in Portugal. He was very surprised when I sent him a letter after reading his book telling him that the same stallion was with me in London. The links were being forged one by one; step by step; Fate was leading Henry to me . . .

The Ambassador was eventually sent to France and his household, of which Henry was now an important part, moved from Portugal. It was an overland trip and Henry travelled some

16

of the way by train. He was a perfect gentleman but the journey troubled him a great deal; there was something about standing in moving vehicles that frightened him. When I knew him I travelled with him on his journeys, but on this journey through France he had to bear the experience alone. People came to offer him a feed and water and he spoke to them as horses do with that soft snicker of the nostrils, but they did not understand the language of horses and gave him no reply. When he was shut in again he made the little snorting noise of fear, and once or twice he used his great voice to make them understand — but no-one did, so the engine puffed away and the journey continued. He could not see the pine forests, only smell them to remind him of the days in the Alpine stud, and the rush of wind in the tunnels made him break out in sweat. He accepted that all this was necessary for his life with man, for like his forebears he could not see a life without his masters.

Back into history and beyond, horses have always been a part of man. Henry's was an illustrious past, his classical movements were used in medieval battle, his blood-line mingled with great names in the history of the breed, names that spell the magic of equine intelligence — Conversano, Neapolitano, Maestoso and many more. He was an instrument and part of the ancient history of man: his aristocratic past had been created by his masters, but his own character and intelligence made him a vital part of that history.

Henry's life in France was at first much the same as it had been before. He was stabled in a fashionable yard and ridden in a large park usually in the company of other horses. Stallions were a little more uncommon here and his companions were either mares or geldings; this tended to excite him and the Ambassador's friends became a little nervous. Because of this one or two influential people caused a change in the stallion's environment. One of them knew a count who ran a thorough-bred stud on the other side of the country and thought he might like to use a Lipizzaner stallion.

The Ambassador was reluctant to let his horse go so far away. He liked having him as part of his household and as he gave Henry some kind of tit-bit nearly every day the little stallion had shown signs of an attachment. But diplomatic pressure was used, and it seemed tactful to let the horse go to stud.

A Lipizzaner was not such a rarity at this stud, but the only other one they had at the time was Yugoslavian and so Henry with his pedigree was in much demand. Sad to relate, his first season was not a success. Most mares had to return and the manager of the stud thought the stallion had been treated in some way so that he could not sire stock; in view of his fine pedigree this was possible, in order to stop breeding on unworthy lines. His life in the country came to an end once more and he was returned to the large stable outside Paris. Sophisticated friends came to ride him and he was an unusual sight in the boulevard doing the passage or the Spanish Walk. People would stop and stare and some made a point of walking in the park at the same time every day so that they could see the fiery little stallion prancing down the rides.

Time was passing, and soon our paths would cross. While my stallion was prancing in the park outside Paris I was running a stable outside London. My wife and I had twenty horses; we had built up a business from Patricia's showing stable which she had started during the war, and this now consisted of showing, riding school work, livery and dealing. We had a pair of black horses in those days, each with a blaze and white socks on the hind legs. We gave musical displays of riding on them and once, the horses wearing rubber shoes, we danced a tango in a dance-hall. We did not know it then but a few years later Henry was to dance in that same hall.

Our black horses were two geldings known as Peter and Paul, and up to that time neither my wife nor myself had ridden entires. In England one seldom saw ridden stallions except in Arab classes and they were from stud-farms in the country. Of course we saw the Lipizzaner stallions when they came over from Austria and accepted them but on the whole keeping stallions to ride in England was considered impractical and unsafe. The fact that in places like Spain they are ridden as a matter of course did not influence our ideas.

Henry had all the stallion beauty, and even to the untrained eye he appeared to be different and unique. He had that lovely muscular crest that stallions develop, and he had the proud bearing and the balanced walk, or march, of the entire. I was later to feel that I had never known the real joy of riding until I had known and ridden this stallion.

18

3

London

Of all the great capitals of the world, London, with its big, spreading river and many old buildings, has the calmest air; the open spaces are beautiful in spring and coming upon Hyde Park at one of its proud gateways is in itself an experience seldom enjoyed in a city of such size. The last link left in the chain, the last months in Henry's life before he became mine, was to be spent in these surroundings. Time is irrelevant on such an occasion; in fact, Time does not exist, only the moment hanging in the balance of eternity matters. When that moment comes it lives on in the mind and becomes the purpose and the whole of life; there was nothing before this because such an eternal moment is with us for the rest of our lives, and forever . . .

Another frightful journey had to be completed and this time Henry experienced travelling by sea. As the sea was too rough when he arrived at the docks he had to spend two days in a dark stable until the weather improved. Even then, when it was decided to let him travel the authorities found his papers were not in order and he was delayed a further day. He was eventually housed on the deck of the ship and one of the Ambassador's staff remained with him as his groom. Henry was terrified most of the time and sweated off his condition; if it had not been for the companionship of the groom he would have been in an even worse state than he was.

Arriving at the dock-side in England was not the end of the journey. His horse-box had broken down twice on its way down from London so when it did arrive it was too late for him to continue that day. It was decided to let him stay a night in a local stable and let him travel up to town the next day. The Ambassador was told of this and agreed immediately. The foreign groom unfortunately thought all British stables were the same and took him to the nearest one to the docks; this was a calamity because the stable turned out to be a small local riding school with no facilities for housing a stallion. The owner was a fairly inexperienced girl who let them put Henry in a box with direct access to twenty little ponies who were living out but had freedom to wander into the yard at any time. Henry was delighted of course and spent a lot of energy screaming madly at them over his door. The final stage was twenty ponies rearing about the yard with Henry teetering over his half-heck door amongst them. The girl and the groom waded in and tried to quieten the situation but not before they received one black eye and two broken ribs.

Poor Henry was finally shut in his box and the ponies locked out of the yard. It was a bad night for him and he was not refreshed the next morning, but his horse-box had been repaired and he was soon made ready for the last stage of his journey. I don't think he ever forgot his travels, because sometimes he would refuse to go into a box as if some appalling memory stopped him. Normally he would stop at nothing; he was fearless and bold and if on these occasions one spoke to him gently he would regain his confidence and obey.

The drive up to London was uneventful except for traffic congestion in the suburbs; this meant a lot of stopping and starting which Henry found a strain, but his new home was to be a stable in the heart of London so the box-driver could not avoid the traffic and when he arrived at the mews he could not drive very near because of cars parked in the way. They had to unload the stallion in the main road, and he was sweated up so badly he had to be walked about for an hour to cool off. At last the stable-owner took him into his loose-box. Like a lot of mews stables it was built on two floors and the horses on the top floor used a cobbled ramp to reach their boxes. Henry had a large airy box on the ground floor with high iron bars and rows of stalls on his left side. He screamed a bit at first and everyone was terrified of him but within one week his character and obedience became obvious to all and he was accepted.

The idea that stallions should be kept separate prevailed, so he was exercised alone, and he was always so much more excited by himself. The Ambassador made new friends and within a short time the little stallion was being ridden by some of London society. He was well-known and admired in Rotten Row and a lo of people thought that as he came from Portugal he was Andalusian. As the Lipizzaner originates from Andalusia the mistake was an easy one. I think someone nicknamed him Henry while he was in London. As he was probably the only ridden stallion in Hyde Park he was laughingly referred to as Henry the Eighth and his wives. To me he was Henry the Lipizzaner and I could never think of him as anything else.

Now the story must change again. The day I first heard of Henry's existence is one I cannot forget. A princess, sister to the wife of an American President, had appeared at my stable and I had just returned from taking her for a ride in Richmond Park. I said good-bye and watched her drive her Porsche down the road when the telephone bell rang in the yard. It was late and I wanted my lunch but one of my staff in the office answered it.

'Oh blast,' I thought, 'I bet it's for me.'

'It's a London Embassy,' called the girl. 'They insist on speaking to you.'

It was the secretary of Henry's owner, the Ambassador, now domiciled in London. 'Can you take a stallion at livery in your stable?' he asked.

I gulped. 'What sort of stallion?'

'A Lipizzaner stallion,' he answered, and he told me to whom it belonged. I must admit I hesitated, but of course one had such romantic ideas about these fabulous creatures that it was tempting ... However, I had the presence of mind to say I would have to ring back.

My wife and I discussed the matter and decided it would be too risky to have a stallion in the yard with the other horses. One had enough problems without creating more, ours was essentially a town stable and we felt stallions should be kept on stud-farms. Friends tried to talk us into having him. 'After all,' they said, 'these stallions spend their lives being ridden in High School and are not really like the entires you know!'

We had not made up our minds before the Embassy rang again. It seemed that for some reason best known to themselves they were anxious to get Henry away from his mews stable and into the suburbs.

'Let's chance it,' said my wife. 'It would be wonderful to ride him.'

The decision, not without misgivings, was made. In my ignorance I made no special preparation; I just arranged a back box with iron bars to be made free and geldings put into the two adjoining boxes. Our yard was very picturesque with a clock-tower, an archway and cobbled interior, but the stables were mews-like with internal boxes and high beamed ceilings.

Originally the yard belonged to the house of Fitzherbert and the Duke of Cambridge, and there were coach-houses, big stalls for the driving horses and boxes for hunters and hacks kept for the guests of the house. The owner of the mews stable in town brought Henry down to us. I cannot remember what he told me about the stallion, but Henry was certainly a thrilling and unforgettable sight. He emerged from his box with a flourish and a loud voice; a lot of tossing mane and he entered my yard with great marching strides. Looking back on that day I realize he came very much as the boss-animal — he was a King and this was to be his home; he came as if to possess it, he showed us the pride and strength he had, an immortal amongst us; but, as we were to learn, an honest creature, a devoted and intelligent friend.

We treated him carefully and after the geldings had sniffed noses and he had boxed cleverly with his forefeet things settled down. It was not so good the next day when a groom led a mare past his box and he reared up with his forelegs over the iron bars. Our boxes were probably lower than the ones in the centre of London and I rushed in just in time to see him balancing on the top. How I pushed or persuaded him to back down I shall never know. Immediately afterwards I engaged a carpenter to build a barrier two feet higher round his box.

'I think he is going to be a problem,' I said to my wife.

'Yes,' she said, 'and now I suppose you had better get on and exercise him!'

My first ride was memorable. I arranged for my staff to take their rides along a certain track and planned to take Henry on another route so as to avoid them. My head-girl, being a very intelligent young lady, presumed I would choose the usual route and to keep out of my way decided to take the other track that day — so of course along a narrow thickly-wooded path we suddenly came face to face! Up until then Henry had been screaming and marching away with tense excitement but at that moment I felt him relax beneath me.

'I'll turn back,' called my head-girl.

'No — no — it's all right!' I answered. 'He's quite settled.'

How little we understand our animals. That first ride taught me that all Henry wanted was to be with the others. Why should he be kept separate from them? He knew instinctively where they were; it might have surprised me to come face to face with them but it did not surprise him.

I seldom exercised him alone after this because I knew by his relaxed manner he was happy to be accepted by the other horses. After all, he was bred with others and by nature he was gregarious; but of course one had to take precautions when riding a stallion with mares. Henry was, we discovered, perfectly honest about this; he would greet them with a great show of masculinity but he would never, whilst under your control, take advantage of it. Later when he became mine this was demonstrated very clearly when my small son decided he wanted a white stallion like Daddy's.

We searched the country for a little white pony with the right looks and eventually found one on a farm in Windsor. I can see Magic now in a vast deep-litter barn, the roof hanging solid with virginia creeper and this ten-hand pony, all white with big eyes, standing in the middle. Unfortunately Magic was a mare but my son did not really know the difference — so his little Henry came home to a great deal of excitement. What was so remarkable was that I used to lead my son on the pony from a grey cob and it was never wholly successful; they both disliked each other and tried to bite. But one day I was on Henry and took over the leading rein. I am positive the little stallion understood the situation immediately, because he accepted the tiny mare and never put a foot wrong. After this I chose Henry for the job because with his intelligence he made the whole thing possible and successful.

Before I owned him I only exercised him and rode him like any other livery in the yard. Someone would telephone from the Ambassador and say: 'His Excellency will be down at such a time — will you meet him and ride the stallion please?'

This I did. The first time the rendezvous was on Wimbledon Common. I was surprised when an enormous American car drove up and what seemed like dozens of people emerged from it. Introductions were made and I rode the stallion in walk, trot and canter. The Ambassador expressed surprise when I cantered him and he told me that some people found his canter frightening. The canter was very exciting, with a lot of head-tossing, but I found nothing frightening about this little horse. One or two young men in the party rode him and one did break into a canter; Henry immediately flung his head down as if to buck — something he never did — and the young man came back and dismounted.

Some people seeing Henry for the first time were frightened, too, by his voice. Like all stallions he had a loud voice, but he used it far more than is usual even for stallions. It had many distinct nuances, which eventually we learned to understand. He would not merely look at something — he would 'comment' too! One sound he always made whenever he was in a situation that he either didn't like or thought quite unnecessary. As soon as the situation changed to his liking — in other words, when he got his way! — he would become docile and quiet. If ever a horse tried to communicate with humans, this one most certainly did.

Meetings with the Ambassador occurred about once a month and on other occasions one or two of the Ambassador's friends would come down from town to ride him out. They were good riders and thoroughly enjoyed him. He was then of course ridden alone and usually he became very hot and excited. One of these people had ridden Lipizzaners and knew the aids for some of the High School movements; this I found interesting because it showed me what Henry was capable of doing. I had owned and ridden a dressage mare who had been schooled to perform turns, passes and canter changes but at that time movements like passage and piaffe were beyond my experience. Patricia and I had shown hacks and hunters but this sort of riding was again quite different. A pattern was formed and Henry's life settled into a routine. I was away from the stables a fair bit around this time so Patricia had the fun of exercising him and he grew strongly in her affections.

I now began a new kind of career. I started stunt-riding for films. I had always been interested in acting, and had produced my own plays for repertory. A friend of mine had a horse at livery with a stable in Stanmore which regularly hired horses for films, and she often met and had drinks with agents and stunt-riders. She happened to give them glowing reports of me, my riding and the marvellous stallion in my charge — and one day an agent telephoned and asked me to report to MGM for work on the film *Knights of the Round Table*. I thought my combination of theatrical and equine experience would fit the job — it turned out that it didn't of course, but at least it gave me

24

further experience of a totally different kind that I would never have had otherwise! I thought this first film would be an isolated incident, but on the contrary, I was on call from then on for practically every horsey film being made.

Around the same time circumstances changed once more. Henry became a permanent part of my life.

4

Ownership

Henry developed a cold and I rang the Ambassador's secretary saying all exercising had to be curtailed. This was difficult because some of the people who rode the horse had open access to him and therefore had to be told individually. I did manage to stop some of them but when the stallion developed a cough I became fiercely protective. He lost weight and his big neck muscle flopped loosely. I put him on light exercise and when I tried to lunge him he disdainfully turned and looked at me; then I tried long-reining and realized he was telling me lunging was not for him because in long-reins he performed beautifully with perfect action and cadence. He was very good about it all and proved an excellent patient.

I was not happy about his condition for nearly a month and when the Ambassador's friends worried me to let them ride him again I was very dubious. They often brought him back covered in sweat and I could hear him coughing as he came down the drive.

One night I checked round the stables and when I went into the livery block there was brilliant moonlight filtering through the high latticed window. I stood still. In the corner box Henry looked like a statue. He was looking at me with his great dark eyes and his whole body was drenched in light. For a long moment we stared at each other, then he gave the soft snicker of the nostrils and shook his head and his yard-long mane . . . I slowly entered his box and touched his neck, he snickered into my hand and stood still. His flanks were blowing and I thought I saw the first signs of double contracting in his breathing. This could mean a lasting unsoundness, something which I could not allow to happen.

As I stood there I suddenly became aware of Henry's

originality for the first time; it was the aristocratic head, the intelligence of the eye, the thought that he was part of history. There was something medieval about him, something timeless; this was the start of that eternal moment that was going to last for the rest of my life. He was the symbol of horses bred for man right through the ages. Nothing could destroy what he stood for then — or now. How long I stayed with him that night I cannot remember; probably until the moon faded into the clouds. He gave me a feeling of understanding; I think he sensed, as animals do, that I loved him and he gave me his trust. Perhaps I was like someone in his past who had treated him with the same kind of respect, or perhaps he knew he was ill and that I was trying to help him.

I acted fast. I rang the Ambassador and said that if he was ridden in his present condition he would become broken-winded. I was worried about him and did not want this to happen. If he was willing I would buy him and he could see him ridden whenever he liked. At first such a suggestion was turned down out of hand but eventually I had my way. When the Ambassador agreed to the purchase I sent him my cheque and in the same post I wrote to the various people who had been riding him and told them the little stallion was mine. There was a bit of an uproar but I had no intention of letting him out of my sight until he was really well again.

The first thing I did was to let my vet see him. He had forgotten when he had last vetted a stallion and asked me to run him up and down in the ordinary way. I ran him up all right but when I turned to run him back again he took me through the yard and we didn't stop until we were both six foot up on top of the manure heap! The vet, who was getting on for seventy, arrived in the yard as I re-emerged covered in muck and Henry with his mouth full of manure.

The old vet examined him and finally shook his head. 'He certainly has signs of lung trouble. Keep up the good work and see how he gets on. It's surprising what light exercise and good feeding will do in some cases . . .'

I got the impression that my vet thought I was mad buying such a creature and Henry did not help by screaming loudly in his ear every time he bent down to attend him. However, the task was started. We put Henry onto a good diet, plenty of fresh air and light exercise, and we gave him a course of mineral salts

27

that someone recommended. Fortunately it was the spring and he was changing his coat; I always think this is a good thing and it seems to help the condition. Whatever it was, within a few weeks his good health took over and he became a changed horse. The cough disappeared and his neck grew firm again, his coat shone like silk and he was bounding with energy. We all enjoyed his return to good health, he more than any of us, and to prove it he set us the task of learning to ride him.

We had a circus friend who had ridden Bertram Mills' High School horses and we asked her to meet us one day and ride Henry. This was a help in a lot of ways because we realized that whereas riding aids might be universal the way in which you apply them is not. It took my wife and me four weeks to get Henry to listen to our aids and the day he gave us his co-operation was a great reward. Passage, piaffe, canter-changes, passes, pirouettes and more . . . He knew so much that I honestly think a lot of it was bred into him but of course all respects must be given to his trainers in the great studs of Austria and Portugal. I think that if you ride a horse every day for a long period you really do become part of him. His reactions link with your own and there are no secrets between you. To feel part of Henry was like nothing I had experienced before.

I remember once giving a display on him and he was billed as the Lipizzaner stallion Elvolotoro. An Austrian woman heard of the display and laughed: 'A Lipizzaner stallion indeed! That's impossible. I remember seeing them in the Great Palace when I lived in Vienna — but this couldn't be one of them!'

We arrived and I led the display with six grey ponies behind me. Henry was always marvellous in a crowd and of course he looked and behaved like the finest of Lipizzaners. I was introduced to the Austrian lady afterwards and she was spellbound. She was still incredulous. 'Where did you get him?' she asked. 'I thought none left Vienna.'

I explained that he never went to Vienna and that he had come to England from Portugal. She shook me warmly by the hand. 'How wonderful, after all these years, to see one of the stallions again . . .' and she burst into tears.

Years and years later when Patricia and I paid homage and went to Vienna we could understand how she had felt. Just standing in that beautiful riding hall, with its white columns and crystal chandeliers, made tears spring to my eyes. Then in the

28

evening watching all those 'little Henrys' performing the ancient quadrille was something no-one could ever forget.

Strangely enough, on this Viennese holiday, we met one of Henry's riders from the days before we bought him. She was the niece of a famous man who had owned Derby-winners — in fact she had led her own horse in after winning the Derby — and we had a lot of fun with her in Vienna. I remember walking back from the Opera House one night and this lady, having once been a member of the Viennese society, said she knew the city like the back of her hand. After we had got hopelessly lost for the sixth time we finally had to hail a taxi!

The purchase of my son's little pony Magic soon after buying Henry fired our imagination to the extent that we bought only grey horses and ponies from then on. We ended up with a stable of twenty-two. To this very day I keep only grey horses; perhaps as a sort of tribute to Henry. I keep his colours too, which were red and gold; and his bridle, which we had specially made, hangs in the glass cupboard along with show rosettes and silver cups.

Film work was taking up more and more of my time and it was inevitable that Henry and my team of grey horses should eventually be part of it — not only film work but advertising and greeting cards too; anything in fact that showed a grey horse or pony. I remember once having to pose under the Prince Albert Memorial for an American Christmas card; it was supposed to represent a typical English family riding in Rotten Row and I met my 'wife, daughter and little son' for the first time when we met at the memorial.

I borrowed a grey pony to complete the group from a local stable. It turned out to be an absolute horror. I was able to lead it from Henry but it still bucked the model boy off; then the photographer wanted a shot of the little boy just standing still. Even then, the pony bucked, ditched the child and dashed off merrily all over Kensington Gardens. It took us the rest of the day trying to catch him! And I sorely regretted not taking Magic with me.

Hardly a week went by without Henry getting himself photographed for something or other. He was in the glossy magazines advertising anything from whisky to wedding dresses. One beautiful shot in *Vogue* showed him surrounded by white-grey ponies with a model girl in the centre wearing a white sweater; she was terrified!

Once we were asked to use him for a famous Hollywood cowboy who was opening a new record bazaar. When Henry arrived screaming and boxing about with his forelegs the cowboy was so unnerved we had difficulty persuading him to mount, and when he did we had to lead him through the streets. The little stallion was convinced that *he* was the celebrity and that all the people were cheering and waving for him, and the cowboy, whenever he could bring himself to let go of the saddle, weakly waved and grinned back at the crowd. Another amusing incident took place on the day Mystic, one of the ponies pulling Cinderella's coach for the pantomime at the Wimbledon Theatre, had a twenty-first birthday party on the stage. Magic and Merrylegs were invited and everyone thought Henry should come too. I had my doubts but was finally persuaded and it was arranged to hold the party between the two houses on a Saturday. I think we ended up with six ponies and the stallion as well as a large number of people crammed onto the stage amongst all kinds of hazardous props and scenery from the show. The stars came to join in the fun and everyone had made carrot-cakes, sugar-buns and linseed drinks. It was disastrous! Merrylegs spent a penny and fused all the lights; Magic 'dropped' all over Cinderella's gold slippers and Henry spat his linseed drink over the fairy queen. We had newspaper and television cameras flashing away and I was amused to see a picture later showing Mystic pinching a sugar-bun from Henry and at least four people grimacing because they had been trodden on by the ponies.

The stage-manager arrived and was horrified by the mess everywhere. He had no idea how he was to get the stage ready for the next performance! There were piles of squashed carrots, mounds of half-eaten apples and spat-out sugar lumps; and the floor was awash with linseed oil. I was told later that in the second house Hughie Green, who was playing Buttons, slipped on the greasy stage and took a header into the orchestra-pit!

Our film work was not without its hazards, either. I doubled for Errol Flynn on more than one occasion and he was always ready for a practical joke. He sent for me when he was making a television series and during the second day told me I had to swim Henry across the Thames. I took this as gospel and we plunged in, not without hesitation on both our parts, and swam across. Unfortunately the land on the other side did not belong to the studio and I was met by an angry farmer complete with shot-gun. Needless to say, Errol Flynn was killing himself laughing on the other bank, especially as I could not persuade Henry to go back into the water. I had to march off at the point of a gun and find my way back, soaking wet, into the studio lot. I was reminded of another occasion working with him on a big American epic when the joke had been on him. Suddenly in the middle of a take he had started madly throwing off his clothes in all directions. We all thought he had at last had a brainstorm — but it turned out he had a wasp inside his suit of armour!

It was great fun riding Henry on film work. While other riders were bungling along at an uncollected trot I would be cantering sedately with an air of complete superiority. My stunt-riding in the beginning was mainly falling off horses in battle scenes; later I realized I couldn't fall off and let Henry go free amongst the others, so I specialized in precise work and scenes in the studios. Falling off horses in full armour was all right provided you were relaxed at the time. One day I agreed to fall off at a fee per fall rather than a fee for the whole 'take', and as we had battle scenes all day and each 'take' had ten to fifteen shots I fell off over fifty times — and I had agreed to take five pounds per fall!

5

In the Dance Hall

We held an annual riding school dance, and the event took place in one of the local hotels. It was a nicely appointed place with bars and a buffet room; the dance floor was large and had modern lighting and a stage for the band. We always had a cabaret and on one occasion, as already mentioned, we rode our black cobs in an exhibition tango. When using horses indoors like this we had to insure the floor and have the animals shod in special rubber shoes. A horse takes to these shoes very well and they give a safe feeling on polished surfaces; if used on wet grass, on the other hand, they can be lethal. I always had a rehearsal on the dance floor in case the horses were unwilling or afraid. The black horses were so remarkable that I feel they deserve special mention; they were good-looking but ordinarily bred Irish cobs and we worked them always together, in fact they hated to be separated. Perhaps this was why they went so well even in the dance hall — because they got courage from each other.

Naturally when Henry came along everyone expected to see him perform on the dance floor, and even I presumed that this would be so. It was something new for him, but I had faith he would not fail us; and in fact he did the cabaret two years running. The first time I thought it would look nice if my wife rode him, and she bought a long black sequinned dress; we had a special bridle made to match and Henry wore saddle-cloth and bandages edged with sequins.

'I think I'll get more out of him if I ride astride,' said Patricia, 'but I'll try side-saddle if you like.'

As it was his first time I thought it would be best if she did ride him astride. I asked the blacksmith to put on his rubber shoes and then we decided on the rehearsal. 'He must try out his shoes on the floor,' I said. So I rang the hotel and discovered they had a new manager. 'Horse?' he exploded. 'On the dance floor?'

'Oh dear,' I said aside to my wife, 'he's horrified!'

I explained to him that a year or two back we had done this before.

'Must be mad!' he said.

'We will get insurance coverage —' I ventured, 'and the horse will wear rubber shoes.'

'How many times will you want to take him on the floor?'

'Just one rehearsal and then again on the night of the dance.'

There was a long pause and then the man said he would have to give it some thought; I argued with him and told him we had done no damage the last time and that had been with two horses instead of one. He went off to discuss it with a member of his staff and I hung on, getting more and more furious. When he returned he said: 'Very well — we'll let you take him on once but if I think it unsatisfactory you can't do it again!'

I thought it best not to argue further. 'Thank you, sir,' I answered. 'I am obliged, could I bring him down on Friday morning?'

Reluctantly he said yes.

My smithy put the special shoes on the stallion the night before and I thought I would ride him to the hotel so that he could get used to them on the following day; he was always aware of new surfaces and I could tell by the way he walked he was aware of the different feel of his shoes. He settled down and I sensed he was happy with the security they gave him on the road. They made very little noise and you felt safe enough to canter on the tarmac. The journey was about a mile and I intended calling on a farming friend opposite the hotel to see if he had a box for Henry to spend the night in after his performance. I arrived at the farm and as I caught sight of my friend decided to call there first, but at the same time the hotel manager also saw me and came rushing over.

'You're early,' he said. 'I've got the cleaners in, you'll have to wait.'

'I'm going over to the farm first,' I answered, 'so I'll come across in ten minutes.'

Actually I spent about thirty minutes at the farm and when I arrived at the hotel I found the doors locked. I rang the bell and waited. The manager was in no hurry to open up, and when he

33

did Henry screamed at him. The poor man opened his mouth but no sound came out.

'Y-you'll go into the car-park and I'll open the double-doors into the ballroom,' he said at last.

'I can walk him through here, if you like,' I offered, knowing full well he would refuse.

'On the carpet?' he gasped. 'Goodness — whatever next!'

We got into the dance hall and Henry plodded round solemnly sniffing at the drapes and eyeing the gilt chairs. I let him get used to the feel and the sound of the place and when I felt him relax I asked him to trot. The manager was looking on with a mixture of horror and bewilderment, and Henry threw his head down as he passed the man and gave what the manager thought was a threatening gesture. Actually the stallion behaved very well and I managed to get enough movements out of him for Patricia to give some sort of musical performance. It was when we were leaving that Henry decided to test the manager's feelings.

I rode over to thank him and as we approached I could see the man visibly trembling; I suppose the horse looked very big and Henry would keep talking and showing off. I thought I would make him bow to the man but as Henry stopped and slowly went down on one knee he thrust his head forward and bared his teeth.

'Gawd!' said the man, and turned and fled.

'Oh well — at least we know you will work in here, old boy,' I said and we rode through the double-doors out into the street. Henry immediately 'dropped' and I thought what a good thing this hadn't happened in the hotel. Actually he did drop on the night but we had someone waiting with a bucket and shovel and I think it was presented to the manager with Henry's compliments. He performed well and was a huge success. The following year I rode him myself with a gold bridle and gold leg bandages and two glamorous young ladies doing the Spanish Walk with him, as the finale, down the length of the hall . . . On that occasion I had left him with my farming friend until the evening's cabaret and he had put him in a box with a peat bed. Henry was thrilled by this and had a good roll, making himself as dirty as possible! I had to re-groom him in my evening clothes and the cabaret was half-an-hour late.

Henry was incredibly adaptable, and when I look back over

34

the years I realize how unique he was. A lot of animals get close to humans and the closer the contact the more trust they can give to the relationship. If I asked Henry to go into a dance hall he did this because he trusted me; if I asked him to walk up a flight of stairs he obeyed for the same reason. He had been carefully bred and broken by people who understood how to deal with the animal mind, and no mistrust had been built up during this period. There are people who say they can break in a wild pony in a few hours, and if the pony hasn't been spoiled or frightened they can indeed do this. Animals want to trust us and it is only after they have been treated badly, or wrongly, that they become difficult to 'break'. What an unfortunate word — someone should invent another!

At about this time we had a number of unbroken ponies to break(!) and school on for quick sales. The ones that had developed confidence and trust were so easy that one could saddle and girth them and mount them in a week; but the ones that had been handled badly — probably by someone who was afraid of them or unknowledgeable in the animal sense — took much, much longer. One little pony had been shod before it was handled properly and had been treated so badly by the shoesmith that it took a year before it would let another man pick up its feet. Once this confidence is damaged, it is amazing how long it takes to get it back. Henry was invaluable in all this; we would ride him out with these ponies and he radiated calm obedience which they appeared to want to copy.

One incident should be related here. It was over a so-called 'unbroken' pony of thirteen hands called Goldcrest. He was a beautiful chestnut colour and we found him living in a kennel, six foot square, and owned by a small boy. The parents had bought him for the child and presumed it would be easy to keep him in the back garden. When we got there the pony was so fresh he behaved like a demon. The whole family had lost their nerve and hadn't the pluck to let him out!

'Has he had any exercise?' I asked.

'We used to lead him up the road every day — but he's got so mad and strong lately.'

'Frankly I'm not surprised!' I told them. 'A young pony needs a lot of exercise and should ideally be kept in a field.'

'He's unbroken, you see —' they said, as if this were a complete explanation for his behaviour.

We let him out and I've never seen a pony rear so much. I had a long rein on the head-collar but I needed it all. He certainly looked like an unbroken pony, in fact he behaved like an unbreakable pony, but we knew that if we changed his circumstances he could be quite different.

How right we were. We boxed him home and within a week he was the quietest 'unbroken' pony we had bought to date. Unfortunately the quieter he became the plainer he looked. All the fire he had had in the beginning had made him look beautiful, but now it was gone — and as for rearing, such a thing never entered his head again! We had no difficulty in breaking him and backing him and he schooled on easily. He was Henry's favourite for a time and I led him often from the stallion to accustom him to traffic.

When we sold him on we made sure he went to a sensible home where they would continue his schooling. I shall never forget how he 'took' me to Henry's box to say good-bye. He often did this on a head-collar, but that day it seemed to have a more important meaning; so I let them blow at each other and snicker over the door and then we boxed Goldcrest up to go to his new home. Henry called once very loudly and as the box went down the road Goldcrest called back. I was sure they were saying good-bye.

6

Partnerships

It was a wonderful life but a very busy one. We were always being asked to give displays with our team of greys; one memorable occasion was when my wife rode Henry and a string of children riding the grey ponies performed a musical ride behind her. At one point all the children halted on the centre-line and Henry cantered in and out of them performing flying canter-changes between each one. Then he did the piaffe while the ponies cantered round him in a tight circle, and then the ponies changed the rein into two rides with the stallion half-passing between them. We did the Spanish Walk as we made our exit, saving the passage for the centre-piece and the audience clapped in enthusiastic rhythm when we came to these movements. Henry adored giving these displays, and he would greet everyone with that wonderful voice and nuzzle and snicker at anyone who spoke or gave him their hand. Cheering and clapping never worried him, and if he was happy with the 'going' he would perform anywhere. I remember once giving a display where the organizers thought a rough bit of ground in a corner of the village green suitable for the 'horsey event'. It was all mole-hills and overgrown tussocks and Henry hated it. I vowed after this experience we would not agree to perform anywhere except on the best lawn!

A sad story came about over one of Henry's friends, an Alsatian dog called King. This dog belonged to an employee of mine whose husband had suddenly died of a heart-attack. The dog missed his master and seemed to transfer his affections to me; being with me meant being with Henry, and as King had learned from his previous master to 'ride' on the back of a horse I taught Henry to accept him in a similar way. We were cautious

37

at first, but it was not long before King could jump onto Henry's back and the stallion did not turn a hair.

The three of us developed an attachment. King would search me out in a crowd and give me a great welcome with both paws on my shoulders, and he would ask to be let into Henry's box where he would lie contentedly for hours. Life was good again for this dog, who since losing his beloved master had gone from one bad home to another. He developed his character again: he had a flamboyant way with him, like a naughty school-boy showing off — with no intention of causing harm. I must say I grew very fond of him, and so did Henry.

He was in the stable for nearly a year and he got to know a lot of people including a group of blind children who came for riding lessons. He would let them feel his soft coat and they thought him the most beautiful dog in the world. 'Let us feel the big dog who guards the horses,' they would say.

All was very well until the day he made a mistake. The object of his mistake was a young lady who had just shouted at a horse for kicking his stable-door. King was fresh out of his mistress's car and energetic; he thought he had to protect the horse and he shot across the yard and made a grab at the young lady's arm! It was frightening for her and her father, not knowing the dog, thought it dangerous; and so he reported the incident to the police. This was to be the beginning of the end.

A few months after this King met a local dog for the first time. He dashed over to see the dog off and the dog turned and answered him back; King was surprised and there was a short sharp dog-fight. Unfortunately someone tried to separate them and got her trousers torn at the hem; she turned out to be the neighbour of the young lady King had frightened previously, and so this incident was reported to the police also. The police were kind and sympathetic and when they came to see the dog he was in Henry's box and they were able to go in and fondle him. Those who knew King did not worry, they were all so sure of his innocence. He meant no harm — but the law was beginning to work against him. There were many other dogs who had similar and seemingly more serious incidents in their lives but they were not reported to the police. It was a case of: There but for the grace of God go I.

King, oblivious of the fact that Man, his friend, was plotting his destruction, went about life in his usual happy and energetic way. He guarded his mistress when she was alone at night and he gave to every one of us all the faithfulness that was in him. Then came the day when he met the same local dog. He knew other local dogs including my own and there was never any trouble, but with this one it was different. King slipped his collar and both dogs shot towards each other. Before his mistress got him back to heel a small child was knocked over between them. It was never ascertained which dog knocked her down but, although she was not injured, she cried with fright. And once more the owner of the local dog reported King to the police. This was the third time; and so he was taken to court. Those who were afraid of him condemned him.

His mistress was too upset to go to the hearing and her solicitor could not refute the charges. The magistrates ordered that he should be destroyed. None of us had thought this possible, and it came as a shock. Hundreds of people signed a petition and his photograph, with his friends Magic or Henry and surrounded by children, appeared in all the newspapers.

He had been reported to the police three times; they had a duty to the community, and so forth. There were many days of misery and indecision for everyone. His mistress thought of him as the last link with her husband, a last wrench from the happiness of the past. He would lick her hand and offer a paw. What was left of that past now in his mind? She was weeping again — did he feel he had to show solace for his mistress in another loss? His faithfulness, his generous doggy heart — he gave it all, not knowing that it was for him she mourned.

If an appeal had been successful his mistress would have been faced with three alternatives: separation, which neither of them could stand again; restraint, and who could keep him more restrained than he was already; or death. She chose the kindest alternative, oblivion, a deep untroubled sleep from which he need not wake, where he could be blamed for nothing.

I was very saddened indeed by all this. Although I loved King I had dogs of my own, and felt the decision had to be his mistress's. Henry missed the Alsatian very much and for months afterwards stared fixedly at any Alsatians he saw in the street. Sometimes he would give a soft call. Our dogs in those days were bulldogs and poodles but now I own two Alsatians and realize what intelligent and misunderstood dogs they are. In King's case I certainly think a misjudgement was made.

Henry had another little friend at this time, my Siamese cat Gina. It was the funniest thing to see Gina sitting almost between Henry's ears, and on several occasions she jumped onto his back while I was riding him in the school. She often sat on my shoulder as these cats do, but when I was riding she preferred to sit on Henry's croup. He was very good about this but one day he gave an almighty shake and Gina, caught unawares, was catapulted about five yards away. She was furious — and seldom leapt onto his back again.

Poor Gina had an unhappy end too. A local gardener who hated all cats actually shot her! I didn't know this until five years later, when we had bought another Siamese which we called Tania. This cat was not so keen on horses but we insisted she posed with Henry for photographs. She seemed to know what we wanted, but immediately the session was over she miaowed loudly and went off to hide. There was a lovely shot used on one calendar showing Tania, Henry and Magic looking out of the same doorway. To make this possible I spent the best part of a morning lying on my stomach making sure Henry didn't bully Magic and that Tania didn't decide it was time to run off and hide! We were only paid for our modelling session and never knew when the pictures would be used by the cards people, so that this way I sometimes missed seeing the best of the pictures and this particular calendar was sent to me by a friend who had found it in an out of the way village shop in Cornwall.

I used to ride Henry bare-back in a head-collar sometimes, just to meet the last ride coming home late on a Saturday afternoon. He looked magnificent, and on one of these occasions we were seen by a party from the German Embassy. Afterwards they told us how thrilled and surprised they were to see such a creature in England. It was the start of many contacts and enjoyable social meetings. Once we were invited to an informal reception and were surprised to find everybody had a title of some kind. There were counts, countesses, barons, princes and princesses. It was considered, I suppose, that our owning a Lipizzaner stallion was sufficient title in itself. Henry was an aristocrat!

7

Film Fun

On one of my first films I arrived by car and was waved ceremoniously through the gates of the studio. This happened several times and I began to wonder who they thought I was. A friend laughed when I mentioned it because the reason was simply that my car was the same make and colour as all the cars belonging to the studio. I was embarrassed too when I turned up on my second film location and the first person I saw being brought up on a stretcher with a broken leg was one of the actors I had taught to ride. I was really a stunt rider by accident in those first films — having signed a contract without reading it I found I was expected to do all kinds of hazardous things! I think Henry, coming along when he did, saved me from a fate worse than death; I found specialized stunting much more interesting. One did not need to know how to ride a horse to fall off it; but one needed to know how to ride a horse to stay on when precise 'doubling' for the stars was required.

I doubled once for Ian Carmichael and during one shot the Boulting Brothers told me to stand in by mistake and the whole company went on strike. Equity members, as I was, 'doubled' and only Crowd Artists 'stood in'. I felt very guilty because the strike lasted nearly two months. In a film called *Yank in Ermine* we were asked to go to Beaconsfield Studios to do a point-to-point scene. This was a doubling job for Buster Keaton Jr . . . I had not been to Beaconsfield Studios before and found it a delightfully friendly place; the unit started at a respectable hour and the locations were all within a reasonable distance of the studio.

'No-one's ready yet,' said an assistant when I arrived. 'Go and grab a cup of coffee.' I found the canteen large and well-stocked and it was while I was drinking my coffee an old friend came in

41

for the same purpose. 'Nothing stirs yet,' said John with a broad smile.

We sat gossiping about old times and when an assistant burst in and yelled: 'Where the heck is everybody — the coach is waiting!' we jumped to our feet. 'Do you think it's waiting for us?' I asked. Unfortunately it was, which proved the bad liaison between the assistants; not that it mattered much because once we were aboard we had another thirty minutes to wait. On this occasion the horses were being travelled separately and after I had checked on my box-driver I was happy to have John's companionship in the coach.

'Where are we going?' I asked.

'A Point-to-Point course somewhere beyond Harrow,' I was told. At least, I thought, it wasn't in Somerset or Norfolk or some such far-away place. We settled down to a comfortable journey and very soon it seemed we were at the location.

'You'll never guess,' said John, 'this is one of the stiffest Point-to-Point courses in the country.'

'Oh no —' I gasped. Although I did use Henry later I decided I couldn't use him here. The master-of-the-horse was an old friend and he had a big grey gelding amongst his horses so I asked for that. Neither John nor I had had experience in Point-to-Point and my jumping had been mostly confined to hunting and show-jumping. 'You'll have to use the proper seat,' warned John. 'Lean back when you land the other side of the jumps!'

'IF I land,' I said.

We got ourselves into our colours and the director told me I had to be third place throughout the shots. The groom led the big grey out to me. As it was a cold day I was wearing a thick sheep-skin coat. 'I'll keep my coat on for a while,' I said to him. He looked a bit wary and held the gelding at arm's length. 'What's up with him?' I asked.

'E's been given a bucketful of oats and 'e's bin in 'is stable for three days!'

'He must be a little fresh,' smiled John.

That was the understatement of the year. I clambered into the saddle and the groom still held onto the bridle. 'OK,' I said.

'Hadn't you better take off your coat now?' he asked. I did so and handed it to him.

'Shall I let go then?'

42

'Of course —'

He did! Words failed me as the grey leapt forward into the biggest fly-buck imaginable and I was galloping down the field with all the wind knocked out of me. 'Third place, he said!' I gasped as I turned in a wide arc and came galloping back again.

The poor old horse was beside himself with freshness and it took him all of three days to settle down. How we kept in third place for the scenes I shall never know because I always ended up first after we had gone past the post. At one point we had to jump over a hidden camera and as we took off the horse faltered in mid-air and shot me unceremoniously on top of the camera-man.

Eventually the director, after examining all the jumps, decided to stick to just one. It was a relief to find he had chosen a brush with a good slope on the landing side; some of the jumps were downhill into plough and others had sharp bends from post and rail or piles of tree-trunks.

I mastered the jumping style and we survived the first day; in some ways it was easier than doing a battle scene and I was beginning to enjoy it. After we completed the distance shots it was decided to re-create the big brush jump near the studios for close-ups. It was done very well but it was flimsy in comparison with the original jump. This I did not mind and was pleased for Henry to have it easier. He always gave a 'cat jump' over obstacles — that is, paused before jumping; it was most disconcerting, and it took us several practice jumps before we started to enjoy ourselves.

We spent several days on this picture. An amusing thing happened at the end of it which demonstrated Henry's sense of humour. We had spent longer than usual in the canteen and I had left Henry in the care of an admiring assistant. We had to wait because we had promised to take another horse in the box back to London. By the time John and I had finished saying good-bye to the unit it was getting dark and as we left the canteen a young boy dashed in, nearly knocking me off my feet.

'Is Henry your horse?' he asked.

'Yes — why?'

'Bill Jones was looking after him at the gate and —'

'Something wrong?' we gasped.

'Well — he's got him in a corner and —'

43

Before the inarticulate boy could say more we heard a yell from the horse lines. 'Help!'

John and I rushed over and were amazed by what we saw. Bill, the assistant — a rather unhorsey young fellow — was on his knees in a corner and Henry was standing over him. The head-collar rope was dangling free and every time Bill moved Henry gave a mild striking movement with his forelegs. It was obvious that Henry was playing a game with the man because he did nothing until the man moved — even a little finger! — and then he made his threatening gesture and of course got the reaction he wanted.

'He's going to murder me!' wailed Bill.

'Don't be silly,' I said, 'you're playing his game — stand up and take hold of the halter-rope.'

As soon as Bill did this Henry turned away totally unconcerned (but I am quite sure he was smiling!).

Talking of horse-boxes — I took the part of a driver on one occasion and I had a scene to do with Maureen O'Hara. When she finished her lines I answered her and then lifted the ramp of the box. It was spring-loaded and shot up so suddenly it caught the star an almighty blow on her back. Henry who was facing the wrong way for camera reasons got a blow on his nose for which he never forgave me — and I was in disgrace for the rest of the picture. Richard Todd was in this film and he was very keen on horses; on another film I remember spending a whole day talking horses with him while we were floating on a raft on a pond! This was for Preminger's *Saint Joan* and although it was a vast set-up with hundreds of rafts and soldiers the scene was cut out of the film because the rushes made them look like models in a studio tank!

We sometimes had to gallop horses indoors, and to end up standing on a precise chalk mark was difficult. Assistants cracked whips behind us to make the horses stampede in the short distance required. This was done in *Richard III* when, at the end of the picture, Sir Laurence Olivier actually lay down and let us gallop over him. He was a good horseman and often did his own shot better than his double.

In *The Devil's Disciple*, also with Laurence Olivier, I had the part of an outrider to a cavalcade. This seemed very simple on the first day but things got progressively worse when the cavalcade had to struggle through deep mud and burning

44

buildings. Also there was trouble with the unions; the Crowd Artists decided that outriders were part of the crowd and that I should join their union. I refused but I think a lot of the riding jobs went to them after this and I winced with horror at some of the bad riding we saw in the film sequences. This is, sad to relate, something that the public and obviously some of the producers don't even notice.

I was often a mounted policeman and used Henry whenever I could, although he was really too medieval-looking for a police-horse. In *March Hare* I was mistaken on Epsom Downs for a real policeman and passers-by asked me what was going on. Also in this film I had fun with jockey Johnny Gilbert; I always told him that with his short stirrups he had no control of his horse and proved this when one day he 'borrowed' my police-horse because his 'race-horse' kept swinging round and refusing to ride straight into camera. As soon as he got onto my horse he had the same trouble, whereas with my long stirrup and leg I kept his horse as straight as an arrow.

In *Quentin Durward* with Robert Taylor we did some battle scenes and I had to be de-horsed and continue fighting on foot. Having had some fencing lessons I thought I knew it all but unfortunately my opponent was determined to cut me down and by the time my knuckles were pouring blood I decided to play dead. The director saw this and thought it would look good on the castle steps, so we repeated the sequence with me falling down twenty steps and then lying on my back with my head and shoulders hanging over a drop of about thirty feet!

8

The First Long Ride

After *Richard III* I was asked by the film's distributors to ride Henry from London to Norwich to advertise the film. The idea was to visit all the cinemas and take letters of introduction from Sir Laurence Olivier to the mayors and mayoresses of each town. This was the first long ride I did in full armour (I actually did a second, which will be described later), and it needed much thought and preparation. I met the company and discussed terms and they agreed to a fee plus my expenses. I then arranged for a horse-box to accompany me; I planned to ride about twenty-five miles per day. I did actually take a second horse with me but the ride was done in icy conditions so I sent the second horse home and Henry and I did the whole journey alone. He was so intelligent and acclimatized himself to conditions so quickly I felt I should be safer with him.

We started off early one Saturday morning from Leicester Square. There were quite a few people about and a lot of cameras, also an outside television crew. Henry was dressed in a caparison and medieval bridle — I was in armour with a tall lance to carry in my right hand. My box-driver, a Cockney lad called Georgie with a great sense of humour and plenty of cheeky charm to go with it, told me which way to go and promised to meet me somewhere en route. Henry let everyone know he was on his way and trod the roads out of London with free marching strides. I didn't think it fair to ask him on these occasions to do anything except an ordinary walk, trot and canter, and in any case he carried himself with such pride he could not help being impressive.

The walk out of London proved to be the easiest part of the journey. We passed some stall-holders who gave Henry tit-bits

46

nd made a fuss of him; he seemed to like his public role and
esponded with enthusiasm.

At one point I became aware of a metallic clanking behind me
ind stopped to have a look. It was difficult enough to get on a
iorse in full armour so I didn't want to have to get down if I
could help it, and I asked some men digging a hole in the road to
help.

'What's loose behind?' I asked.

'Looks like a metal chain,' answered one of the men. I thought
iow funny we English are; here was a Knight in Armour asking
a working man for assistance and the man was accepting the
ituation as if it happened every day of his life.

'What sort of chain?'

'It's a kind of weight inside this rug-thing on your horse,' he
aid.

'Can you pull it out then?' I asked.

He tried but found it was stitched into the caparison.

'Oh blast,' I muttered. 'Can you break it off then do you
hink?'

He tried and found it too thick to break. By this time we had a
vhole work-force of men standing round offering helpful
uggestions.

'Have you got a pair of pliers?' I asked hopefully.

'I think I have,' said one man. He produced a cloth bag and
delved inside it. Out came tea-flasks, sandwiches, towel and
ace-flannel and then Presto — a pair of pliers.

'See if you can cut the wretched thing off please.'

He soon snapped it off and very kindly cut off a yard or two
rom the other side as well. 'That should help to balance things
ip a bit,' he said.

There was a pause while we all grinned at each other and then
ine man said casually: 'Going far, mate?'

I nodded. 'Yes. Norwich.'

'Well I never. What's it all for then?'

I showed him the words on the banner. 'Richard the Third,'
ie read. 'Some King wasn't he?'

'It's a film actually. You must go and see it!'

I thanked them for their help and went on my way.

The weather seemed to worsen as we reached the outskirts of
own. I was getting colder by the hour and I hoped my box-man
vould appear — I felt we needed moral support, if nothing else.

Henry was the least perturbed; if this was what I wanted he was quite happy to oblige. I think he enjoyed the new sights and sounds and he never blinked an eye at anything; he had either incredible courage or just blind faith in me. Loud traffic, trains, noisy motor-bikes, people — he took everything in his stride. Sometimes he would draw my attention to things with his wild voice; another horse, for instance. We met several horses and carts out of London and he found this exciting. I let him speak to one cart-pony which was standing outside a market; the owner admired the stallion and proudly told me about a Welsh cob he had. Henry screamed and boxed a bit, looking all fire and brimstone, and the cart-pony answered with enthusiasm. I thought when I moved off I would have a horse and cart following at my heels but the man soon got the pony under control.

'Have you seen a horse-box?' I asked some people standing at a bus-stop. 'I am sure it was supposed to meet me here.'

'No, I haven't — how far have you come?' asked a woman. 'You look cold!'

'Cold?' I repeated. 'I'm bloody frozen.'

I had no alternative but to keep going and I must say I was beginning to regret the whole silly business. How on earth had I become involved in film work? It took up so much of my time. And then I thought of the money I earned. If I did it full-time, I thought, and the work was spread over the year it wouldn't be a fortune but for a few months at a time it seemed like money for jam.

Georgie was nowhere to be seen and it started to snow; I seemed to be out in the suburbs somewhere and it looked like fog ahead. 'Well, Henry, old boy,' I said, rubbing his neck gently. 'This is one heck of a time.' He snickered and marched on, never tiring, never lowering his head.

I look back on that first twenty-five miles with loathing. I rode on other days under better conditions which seemed no problem, but this first day was an eternity . . . Henry sensed my feelings and he called vigorously when he saw a horse-box in the distance. It was not ours. We passed an office block and hundreds of girls opened the windows and called to us. Someone probably said: 'Cor! Look. A knight in shining

48

armour!' — and the thing snowballed until every window was crammed with laughing faces and waving hands.

I halted, lowered my standard in salute and waved back.

'I'm dying for a cup of tea,' I said; then I wished I hadn't because within seconds a dozen girls appeared with steaming cups in their hands. We had a laugh and I welcomed the tea and the break. Actually this was not the last they saw of me for at that moment Georgie suddenly appeared dashing down the street — 'There you are!' he gasped. 'Drinking tea!' He stopped — 'I've been trying to find somewhere for us to stay the night!'

I was glad to see him and the girls gave him a drink.

'Where is the box then?' I asked.

'In a lay-by and the hotel is five miles further on . . .'

He agreed to fetch the box and take us to the hotel, and the office-girls were pleased to wait with me. I think Henry, who didn't like the box very much, was as tired as I was that first day; no sooner was the ramp down than he started clambering in! 'Hi — wait until I get off,' I said. I swung my leg over the cantle and one of the leg-pieces got caught up and I landed on my back amidst a bevy of girls. I sat there, not bothering to get up, and I'm sure passers-by thought I was being drunk and disorderly.

Georgie lifted up the ramp and caught my beautiful standard between the hinges and broke it in two. 'Never mind,' he said, 'I'll get it repaired before we reach Norwich!'

I was assisted into the cab and we said our farewells. The tea had warmed us a bit and I was feeling less despondent by the time we reached the hotel. It was a nice Georgian house with a long winding drive and as we drove up to the front door the manager came out to greet us.

'Glad you made it, sir,' he said. 'We knew you were coming but the weather hasn't been too good.'

'Knew I was coming?' I queried, glancing at Georgie.

'Oh yes — all the papers have been carrying the news.'

I got down and tried to look nonchalant in my medieval suit, and Georgie drove off leaving me at the door. 'I've got a tooth-brush somewhere,' I said, feeling I had to say something . . .

'Your luggage is in your room, sir,' said the manager. 'I'll show you up.'

I followed him across the hall. Several guests were having tea and as I clanked through they looked up in polite surprise. I was too tired to say anything and no-one spoke, even the manager was poker-faced throughout. I was relieved to reach the bedroom and a little surprised — 'With bath,' the manager said, 'and one without.' I had had room with bath before but I was not prepared to find the bath actually in a corner of the bedroom! It wasn't even a modern bath, just an old-fashioned one on four cabriole legs. Anyway it was a bath and I felt in need of it. Before the manager left I enquired about the stables.

'Oh yes, we have a stable at the other gate,' he answered. 'Your horses will be fine.'

I thought I would leave the stables to Georgie for the time being and asked the manager if he would mind undoing the two straps at the back of my breastplate. He was surprised but obliging. Eventually I was out of my tin suit and enthusiastically running my bath. I thought I ought to hurry and give Georgie a hand getting the horses settled — but I couldn't resist having a bath first.

After the first few inches the bath-water ran in stone cold. I sat in it and shivered and gave myself a good splashing down. After a really brisk towelling I got dressed as quickly as I could before I froze to death. No-one recognized me when I went down into the hall and the desk clerk looked blank when I asked where the stables were. 'Did you say stable?' he asked.

'Yes, I did . . . Down by your other gate?' I ventured, as a clue. He shook his head.

'Don't bother. Where is your other gate?'

He pointed down the drive. I started off wondering what I was going to find. I did reach another gate and thanks to Henry calling me found what the manager had described as a stable. It was now used as a coal-house and poor Georgie had spent the best part of the day removing a ton of coal out of what had once been a loose-box.

'Couldn't you have found a better place than this?' I gasped. I knew by the look on his face that he couldn't . . . so I rolled up my sleeves and started work (perhaps the bath would be hotter next time!). Straw had to be put down and hay-nets filled; Henry had to have a good grooming, rugs put on for the night and the tack needed a clean. We finished eventually and went back to our hotel. Dinner was being served and we were both famished. I cannot remember what we had but it seemed marvellous — and I finished by eating a whole block of Camembert which the

50

waiter had left on our table by mistake. I let Georgie use my bath and once more the water ran in stone cold. While he was making the best of it I went back to check on the horses.

Henry was standing very still as if listening to the strange new sounds. He hadn't touched his hay and I knew he would wait until later before doing so. He had to accustom himself to the sounds and smells of his surroundings and he was not concerned very much with his stable companion. This horse was an Anglo-Arab called Charleston, a very strong and self-willed animal but with a kind disposition.

I stood with the stallion for several minutes and he gave me a sign once or twice that he knew I was there. I put some warm bandages on his legs and gave him an extra feed. 'Are you all right, old boy?' He quickly inclined his head and made a little noise: 'Yes, of course I'm all right,' he seemed to say, 'you go to bed.'

I went back to my chilly room. Georgie was no doubt in bed and as I didn't feel particularly sociable I decided to go to bed also. What a night that was. Water pipes kept making funny noises and if anyone in the hotel used a tap the noise of running water came distinctly from my bath in the corner. It started to snow and a freezing wind echoed round the old Georgian house . . .

It reminded me of another hotel in Corfe. We were on location for the film *The Moonrakers* and it had been just such a place as this. I had shared a double room with my agent. He had awoken in the night and shouted: 'I knew it! I knew it!'

'What on earth?' I mumbled.

'I knew when I came here this place is haunted. I can sense these things!'

'Oh, go to sleep —'

'No — listen!'

I listened and sure enough I heard some very peculiar sounds. By then I was wide awake, and so was he. 'It's over there — in the corner — b-by the window —' he said, gathering the sheets round his chest.

The window curtains billowed into the room and I got out of bed to look. Sure enough, something was moving on the sill. It was grey and fuzzy and seemed to extend towards John's bed. I

51

hesitated but before I could investigate further I heard a laugh somewhere outside. I suddenly realized that the window was at right angles to the one in the bedroom next door and I also realized that the well-known jockey Johnny Gilbert was in there with another jockey. When I grasped the mop and yanked it out of their hands John dived under the bedclothes. 'What is it?' he cried.

'A mop!' I told him, thrusting the thing down into his bed. 'Now for goodness sake go to sleep.' . . .

I smiled at this memory and eventually dozed off. Henry, no doubt, had settled too and was at that moment tucking into his hay. It was a terrible night with freezing storms lashing everywhere. And the morning was icy bright with a layer of snow. I had certainly chosen the wrong time of the year — but so had the film distributors; I couldn't imagine crowds flocking to the cinema in such weather; on the other hand as television wasn't so popular then perhaps they did! Over breakfast we discussed our plans for the day. By eight-thirty the horses had been watered and fed and Henry seemed content in his box but Charleston, being unexercised, was rearing to go. It was after seeing the conditions and knowing how headstrong Charlie could be that I decided to send him home. I felt I would rather have Henry's intelligent companionship, and having to cope with two horses in bad weather seemed unwise. Georgie thought he could take the other horse home and still get to our next destination on time. I knew it was now or never — the further away we got the more impossible his task would be.

After breakfast I went to my room and clambered into my suit of armour. I then clanked down to the hall and amidst amazed glances from other guests paid my bill. Georgie brought Henry to the front door and helped me into the saddle. Guests came to see us off and some wished me luck. By the look of the drive I needed it — it was a sheet of ice and the main road was not much better.

'Will you be all right?' asked Georgie.

'Yes — off you go. If it's impossible and I give up, I'll ring home and tell them where you can find me.'

He knew that if it was humanly possible I would not give up and he also knew that my great faith in Henry would help me to go on. Henry acclimatized himself to the going and we found some grass verges which had only a thin coating of snow. The first hour or so went by without incident and we even had some wintry sunshine to cheer us on.

But later things started to go wrong, weather deteriorated rapidly and we had difficulty standing up against the icy winds; I passed a field of ponies and they charged the fence, the fence broke with the impact and I had six gay little ponies milling round me in their seventh heaven. No-one seemed to be interested even when the main traffic flow was stopped by the fun and games — and I just kept going wondering what on earth to do. A shopkeeper knew whose ponies they were and had the presence of mind to ring their owner. So a little while later a red-faced man with his teen-aged son arrived on the scene. Imagine his surprise to see a Knight in Armour riding a white stallion with a joyful retinue of his ponies in eager pursuit.

'Are you the owner?' I yelled. 'You should see your fences are safe on a main road like this!'

'What the hell!' answered the man. 'Do you have to ride along looking like that?'

'I always do — I'm on my way to a battle. Now, can you catch this lot?'

He couldn't! Neither could his son. They hadn't a head-collar or a feed-bucket between them and the ponies could see no reason why they should leave their new friend. I had to keep going because every time I stopped they sniffed noses with Henry and there was a roar and a lot of boxing about with their forelegs. The situation was not going to improve, I thought, unless someone had a bright idea. Fortunately I was passing a garage and the mechanic came out and suggested I use the work-shed as a retreat.

'That's an idea,' I said. 'Make sure the ponies stay out.' He was much better at controlling the ponies than the owner and he got me into the shed and slid the doors shut.

I sat there smiling as the ponies hammered on the doors. Henry pricked his ears and I knew from his expression that he thought the whole thing absurd. The owner and his son were shouting things like: 'Shoo!' and 'Over!' and 'Git out!' — and the mechanic was giving advice while I could hear car-hooters sounding up and down the road.

Someone came and gave me a cup of coffee and we discussed the weather until eventually the conversation turned to why and where we were going. 'Norwich! That's a tidy way yet!'

'Don't remind me,' I answered — and then I was aware of less noise outside. 'I think they've caught those blasted ponies.'

Before we could go and see the doors slid open and the mechanic came in. 'It's all right — we've got them in a garden next door.'

'Thank goodness,' I said, 'now I can get on with the job.' I thanked them all for their help and made Henry bow to them. Outside the ponies' owner came to say good-bye and we parted the best of friends. 'Good luck!' he called.

'Good luck indeed,' I repeated to my little stallion. 'We'll need it — no sign of Georgie and we're still miles from the next town.'

Of course Georgie had passed the garage when I was inside; although he had seen the ponies darting about he hadn't stopped to help as he knew he was late. He drove into the town, found an hotel and went to warn the cinema manager to expect me. After this he decided to return slowly along the road to find us . . . I was convinced I was going to arrive in the town without him and was beginning to feel worried. Henry was getting really familiar with the routine and he was the first to see the horse-box coming along the road. I must say I was relieved.

'The cinema has laid it on for tomorrow morning,' said Georgie. 'And I've got a hotel just out of town.'

'And the stable?'

'Ah yes — well, now — the stable. It's not bad.'

Henry decided he had had enough — and I must say the roads were getting worse, so I agreed to let him travel the last few miles in the box. He was quite anxious to get up the ramp. 'That's not like him,' said Georgie, 'but I don't blame him!'

I took off my breastplate and allowed myself the luxury of relaxing on the hard seat of the cab. Henry eyed me from the little observation window and when we arrived at the hotel he screamed vigorously as if to say: 'And about time too!' Georgie was apologetic about the stable and I must say I was not very pleased. It was an old chicken-barn, very large and very dark, and it spread away into the distance; at the far end there was a straw bed. Henry snorted when he entered, sniffed at the unfamiliar smells and trotted away into the dim distance. I could hear him snorting away and then he inspected the straw bed. We put a pile of hay in a corner and a large feed. He took a snatch at the feed and then, as if to reassure himself, trotted off into the distance again and had another snort round. I had to smile at

54

him. This would be his first night in a chicken-house and by the look of him he wasn't going to forget it. At last he settled a little and when he did we groomed him and put on his rugs for the night.

The hotel was an old converted country house set in a small garden. The owners turned out to be from my part of London. They had read about my coming in the newspapers and were pleased we had chosen their hotel. Georgie said the press were going to follow me from the hotel to the cinema in the morning and then the cinema manager would escort me to the Mayor and Mayoress. It all sounded as if Georgie had got things well organized so in a relaxed frame of mind I changed for dinner and we had an enjoyable evening with lively and interesting company.

Before going to bed I could not resist going back to see if Henry was all right, and I found him standing very still listening to the sounds outside. I could only hear an owl and some mice scratching away, but suddenly I heard another sound and realized this was a new one for Henry. It was the little sound chickens make when roosting and settling down. There was another barn next door and I was sure it was full of chickens. There was no way I could let the stallion see them so he had to be content with my assurance that all was well. He shook his head and snatched at his hay, but every now and again he would stand and listen.

This one was not such a wild night; just a few flurries of snow and a cold wind. I slept much better and the hotel was very quiet. I was up early the next morning and as there was no sign of Georgie I dressed and went down to do the first feed. Henry was lying down so I guessed that even he had had a good night. Unlike most horses he did not get up when I approached. I think he knew my steps and I could creep in to him, kneel down and fondle his head. I was in this position when someone came next door to feed the chickens. The squawking made Henry get quickly to his feet and he nearly knocked me onto the floor.

'Hi — hold it!' I yelled, then I laughed — 'Now apologize.' Henry lowered his head and I made him offer me his near-fore. I think we were both laughing.

At last Georgie appeared and we prepared things for the day. The press weren't due until ten-o'-clock so we were able to have

55

a leisurely breakfast and I got into my tin suit about half-an-hour before things started to happen. Henry appeared to be his usual self and took all the flash-bulbs in his stride. One young reporter asked me whether I had worked on *Richard III* and I told him one or two stories about the film. We were escorted to the cinema in the town centre and met by the manager. He was a bit apprehensive when the newsboys asked for a photograph of him holding the stallion's bridle; and I must say Henry showed a peculiar interest in him. I believe Henry sensed he was afraid of him and did not understand the feeling. We were then taken to the Mayor and the Mayoress and given sherry and I presented my letter from Sir Laurence Olivier.

Whether it was something to do with the letter or something I said to the young reporter I don't know, but later the local paper carried the headline: 'Sir Laurence Olivier rides his white stallion to the Mayor's parlour' — or something to that effect. By the time the paper came out I was back home again, so was saved any embarrassment.

I had one more stop before Norwich and this was to be a charming Norfolk village with a lovely old pub. Apparently it had been a favourite place of call for Sir Winston Churchill and I was looking forward to staying there. My journey that day was uneventful, the weather cold but reasonable. Actually it looked as though it would deteriorate rapidly as the day wore on, but I hoped not until I reached my next destination.

The village was all I had been told it was and the inn was charming. It still had the original stables and coach-houses, so I was able to pop out to see Henry at any time. Both Georgie and I (and Henry) enjoyed our stay and the food there very much. But the weather broke again with a vengeance that evening and it looked bleak for the final lap of my journey. We did not let thoughts of the next day spoil things but when I went out for the last time to the stables that night I found a hard coating of ice everywhere and the sky dark with more snow.

Everyone was very kind and we were helped on the following morning in all we did. A horsey visitor insisted on doing grooming and mucking out and I had at least two pairs of helping hands when I got into my suit. Georgie looked at the weather and then at me and shook his head.

'I'll try,' I said. 'If it looks impossible I promise I will give up.

Stay with me for a while and I'll let you know when you can go on ahead.'

It was the last and the most important lap and it was Saturday and I was due in Norwich during the afternoon. Everyone waved farewell and I was heartened by their enthusiasm. It had been a bit of a challenge — and now I only had the last day to do.

'I think we'll pack up after today and make for home,' said Georgie. 'It'll be a late start but we should get back before midnight!'

I was dubious but half agreed, knowing it really depended on how late we finished our duties in Norwich. This was my fourth and last scroll to be delivered. The others had all been publicized very well but at Ipswich it was not received so enthusiastically; the photographers demanded pictures on icy cobblestones and the Mayor was 'otherwise engaged'. I believe that owing to the weather people were beginning to think the stunt had gone badly wrong and that I would not show up. This was certainly my impression in Norwich. In appalling weather we approached the city. Not until I was on a good straight road with grass verges and not too much ice did I send Georgie on ahead. I can remember a wide avenue with hedges and detached houses, I can remember the box disappearing into the distance, some light traffic and the endless slog ahead of us . . . It was a weary knight who finally found himself on the outskirts of Norwich City. Henry marched into the main streets, screamed with vulgar energy at cart-ponies, and looked as proud as ever. My standard was mended at last so it was with all pomp and glory we arrived.

People in the streets shouted their congratulations. It was market day and the city was busy; I asked my way to the theatre and everybody was helpful. My relief was great. I felt we looked the part and I thought Norwich was one of the most beautiful old cities I had seen. We rode past the castle and into the market with its coloured stalls. At the theatre the manager seemed surprised to see me — but Georgie had made sure he was there to greet us.

The town hall was very impressive and the Lord Mayor and the Lady Mayoress were gracious and extremely kind. They welcomed me at the door and I dismounted, left Henry with Georgie, and accepted their invitation to a sherry cup. They showed me the wonderful regalia in its glass cases and the beautifully appointed state rooms. I handed over my scroll and as I did so I heard Henry screaming madly down below and Georgie's voice raised in alarm; I tried not to listen but I think he said: 'Stand still you silly great bastard!' Apparently a curious but ignorant cart-owner had driven his pony right up to Henry's nose and Henry had practically knocked Georgie off his feet. I never asked to whom Georgie had addressed his remarks, but the cart-owner took the hint and beat a hasty retreat. I still ignored the noises down in the forecourt and continued to drink my sherry. I spent longer than I should in the town hall and I knew Georgie wasn't very pleased to be left with the stallion. He had made up his mind we were going to return home that night and time was short.

I discovered he hadn't booked us either a stable or a hotel so I agreed to the journey. But not, I told him, until I had had a wash and a change of clothes. This was mostly accomplished in the horse-box with Henry. It seemed an unglamorous end to our journey but once we were shorn of the trappings and the press had disappeared there was nothing left but to grit our teeth and suffer the uncomfortable box drive through the slippery streets to London. What a drive that was. It wasn't until I saw the street lights go on that I realized why Georgie had been so anxious to leave early. All his lights on the horse-box had fused!

'Hi, steady on,' I said. 'Henry doesn't like travelling and this speed is too much.' I scrambled into the back and stood with the stallion; he had bandages and a thick bed but he had difficulty keeping his balance.

I think it was somewhere in the Whitechapel Road we were stopped by the police. I heard Georgie say something and the policeman told him to pull over to the kerb and wait for him. This Georgie did but before I could say anything he muttered 'Damn!', revved up the engine and we were off again. I had visions of police cars in hot pursuit but as nothing happened I presumed the bobby had been unable to get our licence number; it was either too dark or the number plate too dirty!

I wonder what he would have thought if Georgie had told him he had a knight and his charger in the back. It reminded me of the time when I had driven my Land-Rover and trailer into a garage for petrol and suddenly discovered it was the brand of fuel Henry had advertised on television. 'I've got your "lively one" in the box here,' I told the pump-attendant.

'Go on,' he laughed. 'Pull the other one, mate!' And I never succeeded in making him believe me.

We arrived home late and very dirty — and exceedingly hungry. I had telephoned my wife every night, so she had expected a call that night too and was very surprised to have me arrive in person.

Henry spent most of the night lying down and I am sure he was tired not from his long ride but from his journey home in the box. The next day we hosed his legs and gave him a good rub down and he was very soon his old self; actually the long ride had muscled him up and he was fitter for it.

Our ride received a lot of publicity one way and another and we had fun collecting the press cuttings. Henry got a lot of fan mail and his press cuttings filled two large scrap-books.

Apart from these cuttings we looked for greeting cards in the shops showing Henry and the grey ponies. The trouble here was that we were hired by a studio and then the photographers sold the pictures through an agency. To this very day I am still finding pictures of Henry I did not know existed. Last Christmas I found a jig-saw puzzle showing a picture of Henry with Magic and Merry outside our old-world stable yard. I also found a children's book illustrated with shots of our ponies; to this day, it seems, Henry's scrap-books still grow. I can look through them and re-live our times together . . . I can conjure up the sight of his perfect head and hear the soft snicker of his voice.

9

Hyde Park in the 1800s

I am sure Henry had a sense of humour. This seemed to me to be demonstrated often when on films we were asked to do something outrageous. He would stop and turn his head to look at me, and I would laugh and pat him saying: 'It really is all right, old boy!'

We got the very small part of the mounted policeman in Mike Todd's extravagant film *Around the World in Eighty Days,* and this was in the scene in Hyde Park. The park had been taken over by the film unit and all vehicles and pedestrians were strictly 'of the period'. I was a Victorian policeman complete with sword and Henry, looking much too good for the part, was my police-horse. We presented ourselves in the park along with ladies and gentlemen on fiery steeds and all kinds of carriages and coaches in single and double harness. It was an exhilarating sight.

We saw action once or twice and then I was spotted by the Master of the Wardrobe. 'Oh dear,' he said, 'that won't do at all!'

'What won't do?' I asked him.

'Your sword! Why do you have it round your waist?'

'Well — it's safer there for one thing.'

He solemnly shook his head. 'It's not authentic. It should be hanging down low on the horse's flank.'

'That's ridiculous,' I said. 'I couldn't reach it there and my horse could trip over it.'

'But these things must be right. Look —' and he showed me a drawing of a mounted policeman — 'you see? In this period the sword was carried like that.'

He insisted on putting the sword down on a long scabbard and as Henry felt it touch his leg he turned and looked at me. 'It's all right old boy. That's where it's supposed to be!'

Henry didn't believe it — and it was no laughing matter

because when I went any faster than a walk the sword flapped about and kept getting between the stallion's back legs. I glanced round and as I could not see my little friend I anchored the wretched thing up round my waist again.

A little while later, just before we saw some more action, I heard his voice behind me. 'Oh dear — you've done it again!'

'I'm going to let it down as soon as we start the scene —' I answered.

This little charade went on all day; most of the time we managed to avoid the man but he had an unhappy knack of appearing from nowhere just when I had hoisted my sword into the higher position.

'If it's a problem — then walk your horse,' he said once.

'How on earth could a mounted policeman catch a criminal at a walking pace?' I asked. In any case I thought my slow, balanced canter looked much more impressive. Henry entered into the game, he even started to warn me when the man was coming our way and once he turned and poked the man in the back, making him nearly fall flat on his face. 'You did that deliberately!' exploded the man, dusting himself down. 'And for goodness sake put that sword in the right position — I shall get into trouble if this scene isn't absolutely authentic!'

The day ended and I never saw the fellow again. Years later I saw the film and on my second viewing just caught myself going by in a flash — so quickly I couldn't tell whether I was wearing a sword or not!

There was an amusing sequel to this film. A rival company asked the stunt boys to advertise another film on the occasion of the première of *Around the World*. It was one of the most glittering premières in film history; Mike Todd had taken over the Battersea Pleasure Gardens for a huge party. Our job was to bombard the guests with thousands of leaflets wherever we could. We took our cars along stacked so high with leaflets we could see nothing through our driving mirrors — and we started our bombardment immediately after the film première ended and the party started. We discovered that all the important guests were taken down the Thames to Battersea by barge and we decided our best point for attack would be from the bridges over the river. I drove from bridge to bridge, illegally parking in the middle, and hurled packets of leaflets at the barges. People standing by thought I was mad but were keen to join in when I gave them packets to throw; we just took off the wrappers and before they reached the target they separated beautifully and looked like giant confetti. It gave me much pleasure to bombard Elizabeth Taylor who was standing in the leading barge dressed in a flowing Grecian robe. We made sure that by the time the guests reached the pleasure gardens they were all knee-deep in leaflets.

Afterwards we gate-crashed the party, which went on into the early hours, and distributed the remainder of our leaflets in the most important places, including all the loos! I may have had a very small part in the film but someone certainly got their money's worth that night.

In *The Truth About Women* with Laurence Harvey we had a hunting scene to do and the camera-crew tracked us in close-up along the verge of a by-pass — with their tracking cameras actually in the road. Fortunately we never met a police-car and the scene in the film turned out very well. Across country later we had a doubling fall to do for the star and I noticed one of the stunt-girls riding my old Jackdaw side-saddle.

'Does he jump?' she asked. Apparently she didn't know I had once owned him and show-jumped him.

'Good Lord no — especially not in that side-saddle!' I told her.

She went white: 'Well — let me have an easy field then!'

In the scene across country we jostled her into a seven-foot hedge and she shut her eyes, grabbed the mane and urged the horse on. Of course he sailed over with inches to spare. She chased me round the field afterwards and hit me over the head with her crop. This was a happy film and Laurence Harvey, apart from the fall, did most of his own riding.

After this we did *The Gypsy and the Gentleman* and I doubled for Patrick McGoohan. The horse scenes were difficult in this, in particular one which gave me the chance to drive a coach-and-four. I arrived at the studio and was informed that we were off on location at nine-o'-clock that morning. I discussed the scenes with Patrick McGoohan. The first one was to drive the coach with Melina Mercouri's double in it up to the front door of a Georgian mansion. I had driven nothing more than a pony and trap up till then and the prospect of a coach-and-four was a little alarming. Especially when I had the scene explained to me in detail. Apparently I had to drive the four horses at a gallop ound a bend, through a gateway and come to a full stop at the steps of the house.

'Try the scene through,' said the director.

I did. It was a huge success. I came round the corner on two wheels totally out of control — we stopped in sheer fright at the steps because if we hadn't we should have gone straight through a brick wall on the other side.

'Great! Great!' drawled the director. 'Now get ready for the first take.'

I was determined to do it with more control this time, but I overdid it and only came in at a fast trot. 'No — no! Like you did it the first time! Now come along old chap — let's have it again.'

And again and again. Sometimes faster, sometimes slower — but never just right.

Someone cracked a whip behind us and we got a better result. The poor double was being tossed about in the coach like a rag-doll. 'For goodness sake — get it right!' she pleaded once, 'I can't stand much more of this!' — and on her last word we were off again and she withdrew her head too late and got a lovely black eye! I decided the only way to do the shot was to let the horses shoot through the gateway out of control and hope they stopped at the required spot (as they had the very first time!). This proved much more successful except that on the thirteenth take as we came round the corner our wheels locked onto the gatepost and we took half the gateway with us.

Another shot was running after the coach and jumping up behind, then wrestling with the driver and taking control. As the driver was leaving the forecourt and had to negotiate the same gateway and bend in reverse he couldn't get away at a gallop so it was no trouble catching up and jumping onto the back of the coach. Yet another stunt on this picture was what we called the kiss of death. Patrick McGoohan had to kiss Melina Mercouri and drown both her and himself in a lake. I was not such a good swimmer in those days and this stunt made me just want to stick to riding horses! One was often called upon to do a non-riding scene, despite the fact I specialized in riding and had my own horse. I doubled for Griffith Jones once and I had to have a fight with another double and we had enormous fun just smashing up a room. In *The Gypsy and the Gentleman* the coach had to end up hanging precariously over a broken bridge. Also

63

as Melina Mercouri's double couldn't ride there was the job of riding side-saddle in a long skirt! When she saw that a man was doubling for her she stopped drinking her tea and said: 'Ees that supposed to be me?' Everyone had hoped she wouldn't notice.

Henry enjoyed his film years as much as I did, but of course there were a lot of things going on at our stable which were also part of his life . . . There were our two years of organizing horse shows for instance!

I introduce my son Stephen to Henry in the hallway of our home, and
Henry accepts him as one of the family

Patricia and Henry take a paddle through the water-splash on Wimbledon Common

Henry takes his duties seriously as Stephen sets off on a ride with his first pony Magic. The small mare could be led with absolute safety from the stallion

Henry with the ponies Magic, Merry, Mystic and Moppet, the original
team he led in musical rides and later guarded with his life

Magic and Merry, wonder-
ing what it is all about,
prepare to pose for Christmas cards for the first time

Henry partners Patricia at the Riding School Annual Dance

Mystic and Merry, just turned from white mice, pull Cinderella's coach
in the pantomime at Wimbledon Theatre

Henry, against his basic instincts, stands perfectly still while the four little
mares canter round him, the only sign of disapproval shown by his ears
being slightly back

Henry and I perform the Spanish Walk

Proudly Henry and I arrive at Earl's Court for the opening of the Engineers' Exhibition after our gruelling long ride from Wednesfield, Staffordshire

Henry and I in medieval attire set out for Norwich on a publicity ride to promote the film *Richard III*

Henry makes an appearance in a children's annual, in which this photograph accompanies the rhyme:

'I'm gentle, kind and far from lazy,
I'll take you on my back all day
Over the hills and far away
And bring you back, fresh as a daisy!'

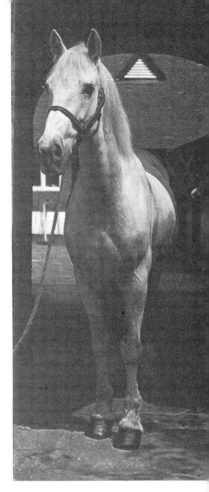

Greyhawk (Henry's spouse), Henrietta and Henry's granddaughter Ella lead another Long Ride to their present home in East Sussex

Immortal Henry

10

Gymkhanas

We bought a pony farm and decided to hold open horse shows every month. We had often felt the need for such a venture — at least, we thought, it would give us an idea of the other side of the fence. The farm was only an eighteen-acre holding, at one time used for pony-breaking and dealing, but it had a row of loose-boxes in a railed yard facing what was to be the show-ring. This we made into a permanent place with post-and-rail fencing and we bought a set of show jumps; it looked very impressive with the rails painted white and the coloured jumps set out in the ring. To make ourselves even more independent we bought tents and field-loos — and found volunteers for the secretarial work. When the organization was complete we advertised our first show. We included a variety of events with plenty of jumping, and gymkhana events for the children.

Entries were slow at first but eventually they made the events look worthwhile. We were to give four rosettes in each class and a percentage of the entrance money for prizes.

The first day was fine and sunny. We had bumper entries on the ground and were run off our feet. With some advance difficulty I had found judges for the showing and riding classes and these had to be given lunches in the secretary's tent . . . All this was fine — but we were in for a rude awakening; we made a lot of errors that first day.

We had held gymkhanas in the riding school where all the competitors knew each other and had a sense of sportsmanship, but at open shows like these everyone was madly competitive and hated their opponents to win! We were sitting in the secretary's tent thinking how well-timed everything had been for our first show and drinking a well-earned cup of tea when the complaints started coming in.

'My daughter was turned out for bad dressing in the pairs!' stormed one mother. 'What's wrong? She's got a tie on!'

We explained that what the judges meant by 'dressing' was how the ponies went together.

'That judge in the best turned-out class,' spluttered another, 'put Bessie Beltbottom first — and the soles of her shoes were filthy!'

'What on earth possessed your judge to put Black Peter first? He's got a whacking great tendon up!'

The jumping was just as bad and the gymkhana was terrible. Seeing the other side of the fence was certainly an eye-opener for me! I thought I had designed the events to fill a gap in local gymkhana planning; easy jumping competitions to enable local riders to get clear rounds and events only open to competitors within a five-mile radius.

'Number 27 won that event — and it was for locals only!' shouted a red-faced man. 'Those people come from Windsor!'

'That's not on their form,' we told him.

'I don't care what's on their form — I'm telling you they are NOT local!'

And so it went on. I had planned to give a High School display on Henry but felt so depressed I abandoned the idea. We went home very tired and distraught. 'Never mind,' we said, 'perhaps next time it will be better.'

But of course it wasn't! I did give a display on the stallion and he went well; everyone received us kindly but it didn't stop the grumbling and complaining about everything the whole day. Henry as usual sensed my feelings and I kept him with me for a while inside the secretary's tent. It was amusing when a woman opened the join at the back of the tent, stuck her head through and started yelling a complaint to the secretary. We were taken by surprise and Henry, seeing the head poking through a hole in the tent, leaned forward to investigate. His mouth contacted fully onto the mouth of the irate woman. She spluttered and withdrew her head and we heard her exclaim: 'Whatever next! They've only got a wild stallion in the tent now!!'

One judge was keen on Arabs and suggested I might like to include a Ridden Arab class. I thought this a wonderful idea because since I had had my Lipizzaner stallion everybody in our yard had become mad keen on Arabs. I also bought the Arabian stallion Horaya, so we had quite a formidable entry of our own.

This proved our undoing, of course, because as soon as we won the class it was rated a fraud by every other Arab owner there. The judge who had suggested such a class was nearly lynched and escaped from the show-ground only by jumping into his car, missing the lunch we had laboriously prepared, and driving like a lunatic out of the grounds.

It was a funny class anyway, because the horse with the best breeding had the most peculiar conformation, the winner of an Arab class the previous week was the worst star-gazer I have ever seen, and one of my liveries had an Arab with a cold back which threw itself, complete with judge, onto the ground and refused to get up again!

Horaya was quite different from Henry. I thought all stallions must be as intelligent as Henry but this wasn't so. Horaya would be very quiet with other horses but, unlike Henry, he gave me no warning when he was going to play up. On a ride-out he would pass an obstacle but he would shy violently from the same object on the ride-in. Of course looking back I realize he was a sweet old horse but Henry had spoiled me completely and in consequence I built up no trust with Horaya. We sold him and he won at the White City after which he went back to the North country where I had bought him.

The gymkhanas did eventually develop into a tolerable routine. We got the competitors under control and made friends with the locals. I think at last they believed our idea was to give them something they wanted and we weren't there just to take their money. Henry proved a great favourite and we gave exhibitions by special request. To vary his routine we incorporated other ideas into the act and at one time had a pair of grey ponies being driven in a white trap with Patricia riding Henry side-saddle behind them. On another occasion we had him perform in long reins to music and we finished with Patricia in the saddle but Henry still on the long-rein. Once we did a quadrille with the other Arab horses and this proved a huge success. We managed to have three greys in the team; later these were used to advertise a famous vodka and then the same team was used again to advertise some non-intoxicating drink — but for this one we had to be dressed to play polo.

The camera crew asked me to show them a few polo shots and I agreed. Having never played polo I made a complete fool of myself, showing poor old Henry as a comedian for the first time.

We charged down the field waving the stick about, missing the ball by yards, and then Henry charged back again, roaring his head off, with a complete disregard for the game. By the time everyone had collapsed with laughter and my face was as red as a tomato I had decided this was one branch of equitation I knew nothing about! We did other advertisements dressed-up for polo but as they were all stills I never risked my funny act again.

During the gymkhana period Henry and I had the occasional film job, and one of these was a television advertisement for a well-known washing powder. This proved hilarious; I had to ride into camera in a white shirt on my white horse and present a packet of powder into close-up. The first time Henry was convinced it was a packet of sugar-lumps and turned into camera so that he pushed the powder away; the second time he screamed with such vigour I looked as if I had the palsy; and the third time he snatched the lid off and the whole scene looked like a snow-storm!

About this time my agent thought he would get me work as a model, and like an idiot I agreed. I thought I should definitely be using Henry, but the only jobs that came along were for me to advertise such things as soap and baked beans. Suddenly I was blown-up on huge posters everywhere advertising some kind of face-cream; I was photographed looking down at a very beautiful model girl and the scene was one of romance and apple-blossom!

The poster was everywhere. I never thought I would live it down, and refused to do this kind of work again. It is quite unnerving to go on the Underground and have a huge photograph of yourself staring down at you; to climb up an escalator and see yourself in profile at every step; or to drive into a car-park and find yourself twenty foot high on the entrance wall! I did agree to one other modelling job which included Henry — but when I saw it I was as large as life and Henry was just a fuzzy out-of-focus head.

We had several television jobs apart from petrol and tobacco advertisements and such things and we did quite a few sequences for BBC films. Very often these were taken in Richmond Park. We met William Franklyn and Patrick Troughton and lots of well-known actors and actresses. Barbara Murray did a sequence with us for a series and we used our old-world yard and afterwards scenes in the Park. We always had famous people's children learning to ride — and not only children. I had a charming lady wanting to learn to ride because her husband had a string of polo ponies; she turned out to be the Maharani of Cooch Behar. It was certainly an interesting life and throughout it all Henry was the personality that kept things alive — even the layman recognized his star quality.

Once at the pony farm we made our own film showing the life of a brood mare. Henry, naturally, played the part of the stallion at stud. It was a delightful film and was shown to clubs and schools all over the country. Our 'farm' was too small to create a true picture of a stud-farm so we repeated shots from different angles and filmed the same foals with different dams. We used the fencing of the show-ring as background to paddocks and of course we had shots of young-stock being shown in hand. This was a genuine class we created at one of our horse shows for the film and we had eighteen outside entries. My son led his Welsh Mountain pony Pride in this class and was very pleased to come in the first four.

We had a lot of fun with the pony farm but eventually we decided to sell it. We were very busy with our main stables; also we wanted to buy a bigger place in the country where we could take our grey mares for breeding. This would have been Henry's and Horaya's chance to be the stallions at stud. We did not know it then but by the time we found the sort of place we wanted both the stallions would be gone — and few of our grey mares were to produce foals.

It was sad seeing the end of the little pony farm, and we never organized open horse shows again. We made a lot of friends during the period and I should think quite a lot of enemies, although looking back at the entries I notice not one of the friends or the enemies missed a show! Ever since this time we have held internal competitions within the riding school and amongst the dozen yearly awards is the Henry Challenge Trophy; our trophies are competed for every year and each one is a reminder of someone or some horse who spent happy times with us in the past.

About this time we went on a holiday to Italy and sent Henry to a friend who had a stud-farm in Sussex. The letter I received from this friend was the funniest I had read in years. Apparently Henry had palled up with an Arab yearling stabled next to him. One day they were allowed out into a paddock and everything was fine until our friend went to get them in again. Then the fun began. Henry opened the gate and went through, followed by his little friend. Everyone thought he would wander into the yard but instead of this he trotted off up the lane. Both animals snatched bits of grass as they went but no-one could catch them and they went up the mile-long lane to the main road at the top. A neighbour rang down to the farm and said they had both turned right into the village. My friend jumped into a Land-Rover and started after them.

They found Henry being given tit-bits by the village constable and the yearling having a good feed off someone's kitchen garden. Henry was very saucy being led back and the yearling was tired out. Fortunately a passer-by took pity on my friend and offered to help, otherwise the task of getting two horses plus a Land-Rover back to the farm which was now five miles away would have been almost impossible. I was sure Henry enjoyed his freedom and made the most of it, and not to be outdone, the next day he broke his stable-bolt so that no-one could get in to feed him. In finding a way in through a window our kind friend got a big bump on the head, and afterwards when Henry was being led out he shot over a pile of newly-delivered granite and my friend broke a big toe.

11

The Record Ride

We were settling down to a peaceful period with good staff and no problems, and we were beginning to think we could take another holiday when suddenly our peace was shattered.

'You did a long ride to advertise the film *Richard III*, didn't you?' said a voice over the telephone.

'Yes — that's right —'

'Well, we have another ride for you . . .'

I groaned. 'Really? Where to this time?'

The voice was very businesslike. 'You will ride from Wednesfield in Staffordshire to Earl's Court, London. Full armour, of course.'

'Of course,' I said weakly.

'You will be the trade-mark of a well-known paint firm and will arrive for the opening of the million-pound Engineers' Exhibition. Could we meet and discuss the matter do you think?'

I hesitated. 'I could — er — meet you in London . . .'

'How about tomorrow?'

Later I told my wife the news.

'Henry will love that!' she said.

Poor old Henry wasn't asked. He was very fit and had been having the last month very easy indeed; so a long ride would get rid of his excess fat.

The next day I arrived at the chosen rendezvous and was greeted by an enthusiastic little man who had apparently travelled all the way from Staffordshire that morning. The whole project was his idea and I got the impression that if the publicity stunt was a failure it would prove his most embarrassing moment. His name was Bill. We discussed the difficulties involved and unlike my previous ride everything had to be

71

itemized and timed to the last minute. 'How long would you take per mile? How many miles do you think you could do in a day?'

I said I thought I could do twenty-five miles per day and that I would average nine minutes per mile. The man then made notes about how many miles I could do between meals per day — miles between towns — time allowed for snacks and how we could arrive in each town at the appointed times. I was to present scrolls to the mayors in ten towns.

We had several meetings in London and I began to realize that this really was going to be a marathon. The man was a perfectionist and I didn't like to spoil his ideas too much by saying that one could not have such a rigid programme when animals are involved. If I had he would have immediately said this was my part of the bargain and it was up to me to see that the schedule was kept. Actually I thought if it proved too much for Henry I could lay on another horse and it could arrive before another day commenced. The route was decided and my time-table made out; I was to have a van following behind me all the time, and Bill was to travel in a car ahead, making sure that everything was organized before we actually arrived. Patricia was to be box-man and would take the Land-Rover and trailer all the way — to carry fodder and also in case we needed it (chance would have been a fine thing!). The whole project was detailed like a military operation and unlike Georgie's hit-and-run stabling we knew exactly where we were to spend each of our six nights. I had two or three fittings for my armour and had to have a dress rehearsal so that Bill could compare my picture with the trade-mark. After this the suit of armour was left with the firm for a last spit and polish and was then to be sent on to Wednesfield for the day of my departure.

Bill started to release information to the press and our first mentions started to come in: 'Medieval Knight's six days in the saddle!' 'Electric Knight!' and 'Six days for the Shining Knight', etc. The night before we left for Staffordshire my wife and I had second thoughts about the whole project; it looked like being the ride of rides! I was trapped in time-tables and had no means of escape; unlike the case of our journey to Norwich there would be no chance to take the trailer any part of the way. At least the weather was normal for the time of year, which was March, so I presumed there would be no ice and snow problems this time.

We had telephone calls from journalists and all kinds of

72

people including an RSPCA Inspector who said he had been asked to put a stop to 'this cruelty'. We gave him details of the itinerary of the ride and said there was nothing to worry about except for the rider! After this we were met by RSPCA Inspectors in each town and my wife found them very useful in finding the stabling booked for Henry.

Our journey up to Birmingham and on to Wednesfield was long and tedious. I was shocked by the grime of the suburbs and we stopped frequently to have refreshment and a breather for the stallion. I never told him he was to be ridden all that way home again ... Eventually we arrived at our hotel in Wolverhampton and set about getting Henry comfortable for the night. He had a large airy stable all to himself; it was a bit lonely and he screamed once or twice — then listened for an answering call.

'It's no good, old chap,' I told him. 'You're on your own. I'll come back and stay with you for a while later on.'

He rubbed himself vigorously on my shoulder and while I put on his stable-bandages he played about with my hair. 'Give it up!' I said. He gave a soft snicker and curled a lock of hair into his mouth with his lips. I slapped him playfully and he then went over to start on his feed.

The hotel was very good and we were given a first-class meal. We were the guests of honour and we had Bill and two of the directors of the paint firm with us at dinner. Polite little speeches were given and they all drank our health; when the evening came to an end everyone wished us luck and success on the long ride to London. I spent a while with the stallion after this and told him all about our dinner party. 'I've let you in for something this time,' I whispered. 'We've got to ride every inch of the way back home!'

Our hotel room was high up and surrounded by trees. There were large nests just outside the windows — this was the first, and last, time I spent the night in a rookery. It was pretty noisy.

Bill was having fifty fits the next morning because my suit of armour hadn't arrived. He made frantic journeys back and forth to the station and lots of irate phone calls. This drama was unknown to us and Patricia and I spent a leisurely time getting Henry ready for departure. We had not brought a groom with us because doing everything for Henry was part of the joy of having him and he appreciated having our undivided attention. When one is near to an animal it is essential to try and look after him personally; in this way the bond is built up between you and the mutual knowledge is unique.

The suit of armour was at the station all the time but its 'loss' caused a drama with the time-table and we were told to get to Wednesfield immediately. I changed into my tin suit — while Patricia tacked Henry up. He had a beautifully embossed caparison and a red leather bridle with red feathers in the head-piece. When I approached him I made sure he heard my voice so that he knew this strange armoured creature was indeed his master.

We were very soon surrounded by hundreds of people and we were officially seen away by the heads of all departments. It was quite a do and we had press and television cameramen following us from Wednesfield into Wolverhampton.

Patricia disappeared ahead and Bill drove off — he was determined to make certain that everyone was in the right place to welcome us at our first stop. I was left marching along with the little van being driven slowly behind me. I reached a vegetable market soon after this and confused Tom, the van-driver, by riding Henry in amongst the stalls. Newspaper-men were there and took photographs of Henry eating carrots and apples from the stall-owners. I came out of the market a different way and had to ask for directions. Tom was furiously trying to find me and we arrived at the Wolverhampton appointment ten minutes late. For the rest of the journey Bill kept an eye on me and when I stopped for a snack he was only too anxious to help get me on and off the horse. We arrived at the Birmingham town hall on time, which pleased Bill, and I made my speech to the mayor. Unfortunately it was the wrong speech because I addressed him as the Mayor of Wolverhampton when he was the Lord Mayor of Birmingham!

Reaching Birmingham was not the end of the job that day. I had to present a special tin of paint at another exhibition in the town. I rode boldly down a one-way street with a policeman on a bicycle in hot pursuit.

'You can't come down here — this is a one-way street!' he yelled.

'I'll rein back all the way if you like!' I answered.

'Hi — stop, will you!'

I stopped. 'Well?' I said.

'Where do you think you're going?'

'Over there — just across the street.'

'With a horse?'

'Well, may I park him here then?' I pointed to a row of cars. It was plain that the affair was beyond the policeman's comprehension.

'That's a car-park!'

'Well — where's the horse-park?'

He took off his helmet and scratched his head. Although he must have suspected I was teasing he was not amused. His mind was full of regulations and he was trying very hard to find a solution.

'Well — you can't park here — and this is a one-way street — you can't go down it the wrong way.'

'Why?' I asked. 'I'm not a motor car.'

By this time Bill was looking out from the exhibition hall wondering why I was late, and he saw me talking to the policeman. 'Hurry up!' he called. 'Everyone's waiting!'

'He won't let me ride down here or park my horse in the car-park!' I answered. Crowds began to gather, there was some laughter and the policeman grew red in the face. 'What shall I do, Bill?'

'Bring Henry over here!'

'But I can't — this is a one-way street!'

'Oh go on, then,' said the policeman, 'and be quick about it!'

I rode on and arrived at the exhibition with a following of people. I had intended leaving Henry outside with Bill and walking into the hall, but on the spur of the moment I rode him up the steps, through the big double-doors, and into the exhibition itself. The policeman who had followed, determined not to let me park on the yellow lines outside, stopped in his tracks and his mouth opened. 'Well — now I've seen everything!' he said, and with the crowd roaring with laughter he got unsmiling onto his bicycle and slowly pedalled away. Henry took everything for granted. He ignored his reflection in the glass-fronted stands and wended his way through a forest of mechanical exhibits. We presented our special tin of paint and had our photographs taken by half-a-dozen cameramen, then I rode the stallion out again into the street. There was no policeman and in any case I was now going the right way and I hoped I would not get lost again.

We arrived at our stable and Henry was pleased to find he was sharing it with a gelding. He settled in very well and I went off to the hotel for a much needed bath. But oh dear — yes, you've guessed — it was stone cold. We rang down and spoke to Bill, who was furious. He had us removed straight away to another room where the water was hot. I was for some reason very stiff and had a pain in the right side of my back, and unfortunately the hot bath did not improve it. Patricia was busily massaging my back when a maid came in to prepare the beds. She took one look at my suit of armour on one bed and my naked body on the other and in utter confusion beat a hasty retreat.

The next day we stopped for a meal at a very busy public-house and were amused by the reactions from people in the restaurant. At the sight of a man in full battle armour eyes were hastily averted in typical British fashion so as not to appear rude or unnecessarily curious. A reporter came into the pub and asked self-consciously: 'Have you seen a knight in armour round here?' and the landlord, without raising an eyebrow, answered: 'Yes, he is in the restaurant.' Later when I was photographed at various stages of my meal a few guests showed interest and one or two actually smiled when I drank my beer through a straw. I discovered I was near a window and suddenly became aware of a crowd of faces pressed against the glass. Fortunately the newspapers had warned people of my approach so I don't think they thought I was just a crazy eccentric.

The most open curiosity was expressed by a group of American tourists. They had their photographs taken in front, behind, together and singly with the Knight on his White Charger. I could imagine them telling the story back home: 'In lil' ole England, wadya know, we was walking along a country lane when look who came by!! Why! A real Knight in shining armour!' At first I thought they were going to believe that some of us still rode about like that!

Owing to this and other incidents on the way we were late arriving in Coventry. The newspapers said things like: 'The Knight was late!', 'Late knight extra!' and 'Another ride through Coventry!' — but that of course was on the following day.

We were welcomed by the Lord Mayor and Lady Mayoress who graciously accepted their scroll — and I made sure I said the right speech. Later the Mayoress showed us round the town hall, including the newly appointed room which she had so beautifully prepared and furnished for the visit of Her Majesty the Queen on the following Friday. We realized after Coventry how much publicity the papers were giving us and our welcomes became much more boisterous. As we rode towards Leamington I noticed a much more friendly approach from the passers-by. There was none of the reticence we had experienced previously and I think this was because they had been warned and there was no embarrassment in the surprise. I felt that Henry recognized this a little and he responded accordingly. He was so pleased to greet everyone, and I allowed him to do his own party-piece, the Spanish Walk, as we entered the town.

Imagine my surprise when we learned that most schools had been given the afternoon off! The crowds outside the town hall were enormous. It was a lot of fun and when we met and tried to speak to the Mayor the cheering was deafening. One reporter said: 'Will your horse mind?'

'Mind?' I laughed. 'Just look at him. He loves it!' And the young man had to admit Henry was showing no signs of distress, on the contrary he was responding to the cheers with obvious joy. 'He was used in the bull-ring,' I said. 'He knows it's all adulation for him and he is proud to accept it!'

The little stallion roared and snickered, took tit-bits from the crowd, and allowed people to press against his chest and play with his tail. He didn't murmur when I put a small child in front of the saddle with me and he stood on the town hall steps and, with ears pricked, surveyed the crowd, tossing his great mane over his enormous eyes. The newspapers then claimed: 'The Knight's horse was a friend of the children'; and: 'The Knight's stallion thought he was back in the bull-ring.' It was typical of Henry's remarkable personality that he was fast becoming the star attraction and I was more than willing to take a back seat. As newspapers warned hotels on the route that a knight in shining armour would be visiting them on his Lipizzaner stallion, people discovered which hotel and we were greeted by a crowd every time we arrived.

At Leamington we arrived at our hotel followed by about five hundred children. The hotel was a beautiful old-world inn, and riding under an archway into a cobbled yard you came upon a picture of an old hostelry. Inside there were lovely oak floors and old oak furniture. Henry had a super stable and I think he liked having the sound of a chiming clock to remind him of our own yard at home. The porter closed the big gates and we waved to the children.

From then on we had a wonderful welcome everywhere. Unfortunately I was becoming very sore and as a result of the rigidity of my armour suit I had muscular pains in the back. At the end of the day I could not slump or relax in the saddle and by the time we found the town halls and the hotels I realized we were doing far more than the twenty-five miles agreed upon in the beginning. But if I was suffering, at least Henry was not. How he managed it I didn't know; he was as fit as a fiddle and would arrive gleefully at our next appointment with vulgar energy and delight.

Bill was a clock-watcher, and time, speed and distance were his constant anxieties. If they became unrelated it was extremely difficult to rectify them; not only in arriving on time but to fit in the necessary stops en route.

One stop we had was at a dubious road-side pub; it was either that or nothing for another five miles. Patricia had missed us and we had lost two newspaper reporters so we were more or less on our own when we stopped in the forecourt — the horse, the van and the PRO's car. Immediately the pub doors burst open and a jovial gentleman fell out. From the ground he eyed me solemnly, and I did one of my statue-freeze positions. 'Gawd!' he said, his eyes popping out of his head. 'Ish thish what it's like out here? Where the hell am I?' He was certainly very drunk and the sight of us had not helped him. Just when he was about to scramble away on all fours the proprietor came out.

'Oh — it's the Knight! Welcome, sir!' he said, then to the man on the ground: 'Get out of here before I get the rest of the Army here!' The poor man did not need a second bidding and the proprietor roared with laughter. 'He's always like that at this time of the day.' He proceeded to help me down from Henry and got a nice hit on his chin from my breast plate. 'How on earth can you stand this tin suit?' he asked, dabbing a spot of blood with his handkerchief. I told him I was beginning to think it was part of me and that I couldn't stand up without it! Other people came from the pub to help and one horsey young man from a local stud asked to hold Henry for me while I went inside. We had a first-class lunch with excellent company and the horsey fellow was so taken with the stallion I knew he would remember that day for the rest of his life.

Our next appointment was Warwick — and we arrived on time. Lucky we did, because ITV were waiting to film us for the next news bulletin. We were greeted by cheering girls from the Preparatory School and they escorted us to the town hall with the film cameras rolling ahead of us all the way. It all looked good with a background of Warwick castle, and Bill took publicity shots of Henry in the pose displayed on the side of his van. Actually this depicted a horse in Levade, but as I could not impose the strain of this movement on Henry when he had so much riding to do most of these pictures were ground shots with me carrying my sword high above my head. It looked very real and all the cameramen were happy with the shots they took. We had our usual welcome here and once again it was all due to our advance publicity in the press and from then on in the television news.

Patricia found the Land-Rover and trailer a bit of a problem. She was never very expert at reversing it and every time we needed her on the route we always saw the trailer disappearing in the opposite direction. The trouble was that by the time I had ridden round a town, found the town hall, and negotiated traffic (and one-way streets), the rendezvous had to be changed. 'Why on earth don't you stick to where you said?' she would demand. This happened outside Warwick . . .

'I never know where I'm coming from,' I answered. 'The trouble is you are always going in the wrong direction.'

'I can't be psychic!' she retorted. 'And I have to go miles before I can find a space big enough to turn round in!'

We all laughed at this, which made her angry. At the time she was facing North when we wanted to go South, so as she drove off again in search of her big turning space we saluted and waved her on her way.

Our next stop was Banbury and we arrived in the evening when the homeward-bound traffic was at its densest. Bill did a good job here in getting us through to the town hall: he got us a police escort! Henry loved this and marched proudly through the streets — I am sure he thought he was visiting Royalty or something. Actually we were greeted in a most royal fashion at the town hall and the Mayoress gave us delicious Banbury cakes with our sherry. Henry stood outside surveying the crowd and was photographed without me for the first time. This was his moment, and the newspapers the next day made the most of it.

What a long road it was. Even after hot baths the muscular pains in my back were still agonizing. I discussed this with a guest in a hotel and he said that even in the Middle Ages no-one rode so many miles in full armour.

'But surely — they had no alternative,' I said.

'They would ride many miles in leg-pieces and a coloured tabard,' he said. 'But the heavy pieces such as the breastplate were always carried by a steward and only put on when they got to the battlefield!'

This sounded plausible. 'So I am doing something that has probably never been done before?'

'Why — yes,' he answered. 'Definitely! You should get your PRO to carry your breastplate until you arrive at your destination.'

I did test Bill on this point — but although he was sympathetic he was not enthusiastic. 'This has got to be an endurance test,' he argued. 'We must try and keep up the symbol of the Armoured Knight riding all the way.'

I thought: 'Well, I am almost there — why try to change things now?' But I said: 'Couldn't I just forego the breastplate for one day to see how I get on?'

Bill knew I was trying it on and shook his head. 'I would rather not, old boy . . .'

I grinned. 'Oh well, when I die in the attempt, make sure I have recognition for the feat!'

Henry was truly the hero, and he grew fitter every day. I kept the work fairly slow and regular, and when I thought he had done enough I sent him off to his stable and finished my job from the Mayor's parlour either on foot or by car. It was the extra miles we did in the towns that made the days too long. I could see no way of cutting them down, especially as I had no previous knowledge of the city streets. Often we were asked to meet a photographer or a TV crew at a certain spot at a certain time, and this could mean a detour back from the town hall; if our hotel and the stables were in other directions, as much as six miles could be added to our daily total. This was where Patricia's horse-trailer was needed — and when it appeared it was invariably going in the wrong direction. We did solve a few of

80

these troubles but the problem in one town was never identical to the problem in the next.

A charming highlight to our journey out of Banbury was the meeting with another Lipizzaner stallion. A gentleman in a Rolls Royce stopped and waved us down.

'I see you have a very beautiful horse,' he said. 'I read in the papers that he is a stallion from Lipizza — and I can see he is a fine example of the breed.'

I made Henry bow to him and the man was delighted. 'You must come and see my stallion,' he said, 'they are probably related!'

It turned out that they were. I followed the man down a long drive to his stud-farm. The stallions roared at each other, and seeing them greet each other made a wonderful sight. I wished I could have stayed longer but I knew I could not . . . 'Come and see us in London some time,' I said.

Arriving at Oxford was a calamity. The police refused to let me ride up to the town hall in case it caused traffic congestion, the Mayor was unavoidably detained at a function, Patricia ran over a dog — and Henry had a loose shoe!

The first thing was to get the scroll delivered. We left Henry on the outskirts of the town surrounded by a fast-gathering crowd and I drove to a car-park near the Mayor's parlour. As I had to walk quite some way my presence on foot caused more traffic congestion than if I had been mounted. Amidst a dozen photographers I placed the scroll in the Mayor's letter-box and then stepped back into the road. Somehow I tripped over the kerb-stone and fell head-long in front of a bus. People rushed to help and after several agonizing moments I was put back on my feet. My walk back was tedious to say the least — and to cap it all, I forgot where I had parked the car!

Bill saved the day by appearing just when I was about to give up and he guided me to the car-park. As I got into the car my visor slammed shut and would not be raised again; I was practically blinded and half-suffocated by the wretched thing, and had to stay like it until we got out of the town. Henry was so packed into a crowd I couldn't reach him — and I pleaded with Bill to find a mechanic to release my visor.

We drove into a garage and Bill asked the white-faced youth

at the pumps: 'Have you got a pair of pliers or something — my friend here can't get out of his helmet!'

The youth bent down and looked into the car. He was silent straight-faced and completely lost for words. 'Er — helmet?'

'Yes, helmet — stuck!'

I mumbled something and when the youth heard a voice coming from the suit of armour he fled into the workshop. ' 'Ere —' we heard him say, 'come quick — there's a geezer in a suit of armour and 'e can't get out!'

A mechanic did eventually release the visor and I was free again. I walked very forcefully through the crowd and I could tell Henry was relieved to see me. Patricia and Tom were there, and Patricia was in tears. 'What's up?' I asked.

'She ran over a dog,' said Tom. 'It's quite upset her.'

Apparently the dog was not badly injured but the shock was too much for Patricia. We got someone else to drive the trailer that night and I would not let Henry do any more miles. Oxford was not our happiest call. The stable was too far away from the hotel and the stallion badly needed a blacksmith. For once the RSPCA Inspector was not hovering round to help, so we had to search for a smithy in the yellow pages of the telephone book.

'Aw yes,' answered a feminine voice. 'The smithy could do something tomorrer.'

'He couldn't oblige us tonight?' asked Bill.

'Aw no — he goes to the club tonight.'

'How soon could he shoe our horse tomorrow?'

'Well . . . he wants to go and see the Knight on his Lipizzaner stallion tomorrer morning —'

'This is the Lipizzaner stallion!' exploded Bill. There was a long silence. 'Did you hear?' he asked.

There was no reply — then the woman giggled. 'You can't pull my leg like that!'

Bill was very persuasive and then the woman went off and told her husband. Several minutes later the blacksmith himself came on the line.

'Does the stallion want new shoes then?'

Bill looked at me and I nodded. 'If he can do the job tonight let's have new shoes all round,' I told him.

'Well — now —' drawled the smith. 'Could you bring him to the forge right away?'

Yes, we could. Tom agreed to drive the Land-Rover and

trailer and after I had had a shower and changed Bill and I drove down to the forge to supervise.

The blacksmith was about sixty-five years old and his shop was well organized. He had an assistant who came in specially for the job and he made the shoes while we waited. Henry stood like a lamb eyeing everything that was done for him and sniffing at the tools as if to give them his approval. We talked about the stallion's life in Portugal and his life in films; the blacksmith was genuinely interested and pleased to shoe the horse and he was particularly happy as this would be his first Lipizzaner stallion. I thought no doubt he would have something to tell his club that night.

Before we left a stray newspaperman discovered us and of course a photograph had to be taken for the local press. 'Ah! Fame at last,' said the blacksmith.

We took Henry to his stable and I stayed with him for about an hour. Bill went back to the hotel in the Land-Rover and left me the car. I took my time grooming and rugging the little stallion and he appreciated my attention. I gave him his stuffed hay-net last and as I turned to go he came over and rubbed his head on my chest. It was a gesture of thanks.

'You're a funny old thing,' I said. 'I must go now or I shall ruin my dinner.' I let him rub his head for a moment longer and then he went back to his hay. I looked at him and I remembered the night in his stable at home when I had watched him standing bathed in moonlight. I have a theory that all animals could develop their intelligence towards us if only we could live closer to them. We ride our horses, we feed and we groom them; then we leave them and come back the next day; a dog can come with us, can actually sleep at the foot of our bed, and it is only like this that an animal can become conscious of our reactions and thoughts.

I returned to the hotel and found Patricia only a little less distraught. Her accident was all the more dreadful for her because of her love for animals, and although hitting the dog had not been her fault she blamed herself without mercy.

We spent a comfortable night after all our calamities and awoke fresh for another day. I rang home and found everything trouble-free; my agent had telephoned to discover if I was still in the land of the living and to say that Henry and I were wanted for another film; two newspapers had asked permission to come and photograph Henry's return — and Harry Secombe's children had started to learn to ride! 'I'll be home within three days,' I told them. 'Henry is fit — even if I am not!'

It was a long ride to High Wycombe but everything went according to plan. Bill was really doing a marvellous job. At High Wycombe we were able to stable Henry with some friends. I hadn't seen their stable and found it interesting; it was a large yard surrounded by brick and wooden loose-boxes, the whole complex set in about thirty acres. Unfortunately the land was divided by a railway-line and to reach some paddocks one had to go under the line through an embankment. Henry was very good with trains and apart from a curious stare at the first one he settled in well. The only thing that happened was that he let himself out of the box in the night and spent about four hours sorting out the hay-barn. He sampled nearly all the bales of hay and distributed a lot of it over the yard. Like a naughty boy he must have dragged two or three bales over to the ponies' paddock where they all apparently had a midnight feast. Two yearlings on the other side of the railway line broke through their gate and joined in the fun. Fortunately my friend started very early in the morning so had sorted things out before I arrived.

I changed into my armour at the stable and after saying good-bye and making Henry apologize for being such a bad guest we started out on the last cruel lap to London. As traffic built up Tom found driving the van very tedious indeed. We met a road-surfacing vehicle belching flame — the buses became red ones and we realized that as the countryside became less and less London was getting nearer and nearer.

We received a great welcome at Ealing and when the local press discovered that I used to live near there they went down Gunnersbury Avenue to photograph the very house. I refused to ride Henry down there just for a photograph and I never knew whether it was printed in the paper.

We all agreed to rendezvous at Kensington town hall. Kensington! What a lovely thought. The journey was nearly over; before we attended the opening ceremony of the Engineer's Exhibition at Earl's Court I could nip home and have a night in my own bed. I asked Patricia to meet us early so that we could leave the others in their Kensington hotel and take Henry home to his own stable for the night.

A lot was to happen before then. The journey on was extremely tiring. I negotiated traffic much better than my van-driver and did actually lose him some of the way. We had TV cameras popping up at Hammersmith and I was grateful for the company of an enthusiastic newspaperman for about two miles. Tom caught up with me in Kensington High Street but then had difficulty keeping behind me. He did three U-turns which brought the police onto the scene, and in the middle of all this I saw an old friend complete with shopping-basket walking along the pavement. Unfortunately she was surprised enough to see me to stop to talk.

'What on earth are you doing here?' she asked.

'Riding to Earl's Court, actually,' I answered, hoping she would not want a lengthy explanation. 'For God's sake, keep moving!' hissed Tom as he passed me for the fourth time. I realized that although London did not frighten me poor Tom, having lived in Staffordshire all his life, was utterly lost and bewildered.

'I must go — I have to meet the Lady Mayor,' I said and left my friend gaping on the pavement.

At that moment, to add to my confusion a burly policeman came over and stopped me. He didn't say: 'Now wot's all this 'ere then?' but it sounded awfully like it to me.

'You're causing an obstruction,' he said.

'Oh — am I?'

'That's your van over there?'

I stole a look at Tom doing another U-turn in Kensington High Street and shook my head. 'Never seen him before, Officer,' I said.

'It's my belief you're on the same publicity stunt and I am going to book you.'

'W-what for?'

'For obstruction.'

Henry roared with indignation into the policeman's ear, which made him drop his notebook, and while he bent down I wondered whether to make a run for it. I saw Bill trying to attract my attention and I saw Tom also talking to a policeman and thought better of it. My wife trying to be punctual as promised at that moment appeared driving frantically in her usual opposite direction and I wondered how far into London she would have to go before finding a big enough turning-space for the trailer.

'Please, Officer,' I said. 'I have an appointment with the Lady Mayor and I mustn't be late.'

Laboriously the policeman wrote in his notebook . . .

'Your name? . . . Your address?' Date . . . Time . . .

'Oh my goodness! Is that really the time?'

12

Battle Scenes

The papers next day — and some that evening — had a field day: 'Ye Knight is in ye spot!' — 'PC catches the Knight!' — '140 miles — then booked!' But the misunderstanding was cleared up and I was accepted on 'official business'. We were received at the Town Hall and welcomed to London after completing the 140 miles from Wednesfield in six days. The national press coverage extended as far as Glasgow and Newcastle-upon-Tyne. But at that moment I knew we had one more day to go — an easy one, though with a strict time-table. I was eagerly waiting for a sight of Patricia with the trailer. We said good-bye to the Lady Mayor and gathered in a back street to escape some of the crowd. 'Keep an eye open,' I told Tom. 'Don't let her drive past!'

He did a good job. He caught her just hesitating at the entrance to a one-way street, nipped in beside her and guided her to where we were waiting. It was a delight to go home for one night. Bill felt guilty not having us as his guests in the hotel but he understood our eagerness to go.

Henry entered the yard with a great flourish; the boss-animal again. He told everyone he had been working hard and that he had visited some important places; and all his stable-companions showed suitable admiration. It was not long before the Siamese cat sat on his shoulder and the dogs shared his bed. The ponies, Magic and Merry, looked with ears pricked towards their hero's box and my staff were soon waiting on him hand and foot.

As the exhibition opened early the next day Bill had thought it better to arrive in Kensington the night before. This meant the last day of our journey was to be an easy one, as I have said — and how enjoyable it was to arrive at our destination, for once, fresh and clean!

Henry was keen and lively and danced his way to Earl's Court.

Patricia drove off into the distance and Tom took up his usual rear-guard position. It was our moment. Crowds gathered on that last morning, cameras clicked and we were filmed by ITV cameramen for our final appointment. Everything was great — Henry knew that this was what it was all about and he let everyone make a fuss of him. I made our entry into the forecourt of Earl's Court and officials came to join in the fun.

I was aware of a man hovering in the background and finally Bill came and whispered: 'It's the RSPCA Inspector. He wants to inspect your horse — see if he is any the worse for his journey!' 'Let him come then,' I said. As the man hesitatingly approached the stallion Henry turned and roared with crude energy in his face. The man stopped, and I was sure the fit little stallion would have been insulted if he had examined him. 'Thank you, sir,' he said. 'I can see he is none the worse! I don't need to look closer!' I left Henry enjoying the adulation and walked into the exhibition hall. I told Tom to find Patricia after the excitement had died down and to load Henry up and take him home. I was introduced to a number of people and eventually Bill and I escaped to have lunch together. It was my intention to change out of my armour and get Bill to drive me home — but suddenly we had an urgent message from the BBC.

Would the Knight go to the Lime Grove TV Studios at once? Bill was very excited and couldn't wait to drive me, complete with my suit of armour, to the studios. It really was for the last time I had to don my helmet — for an appearance on an evening programme. It was called 'Highlight' and followed the six-o'-clock news. The interviewer was a man who, many years later, was to become my local MP. After a test it was decided that I should 'freeze' with the visor down until he spoke to me, then come to life! I prayed the visor wouldn't get stuck, but later when I was on the air I thought how funny it would have been if it had.

But it didn't — and the interview went off very well. I only wished that Henry who had carried me so gallantly all the way could have shared the limelight; I was putting him back into his stable after all he had done, when he had a right to be at my side. And when eventually the ride was recorded in the *Guinness Book of Records* it was again the man who achieved a ride in full armour, never recorded before, not the horse who carried him.

The following year I was asked to advertise the firm again by coming down from Wednesfield, the modern way, by plane! I did this stunt because it was well paid. The light plane from Wednesfield to Birmingham was an experience for me; I was wedged in the second seat in full armour and I noticed the control panel was held together with paper-clips! I am never happy in the air and when it was over I said I preferred the journey on horseback. Next to my dislike of flying is, I am sure, going under water because when it was suggested the next year I came up the Thames in a submarine, I flatly refused!

Before the opening of the exhibition that second year we stayed the night at the Waldorf Hotel. In the lift on arrival the attendant said without even a smile: 'Which floor, sir?' 'The sixth!' I answered. We did not exchange another word and when I got out I had a porter bring in my luggage. He was equally poker-faced; I must say I was full of admiration for the way the staff accepted my medieval dress!

The next morning, in full battle armour, I rode to Earl's Court on a motor-bike, and never having ridden one before kept in the same gear all the way. The machine was red-hot by the time I got there. It carried me, complete with glamorous model girls on the pillion, until it stopped and no amount of coaxing would start it again. I was much more at home with a horse!

Soon Henry and I started another film job. It was a big MGM epic with Errol Flynn, and we had some hazardous battle scenes to do, some in close-up, at the incredible castle mock-up sited on the studio lot. I became so confused with doubling for the stars on the French side and then doubling for stars on the English side that in the battle scenes I never knew which side I was on! Eventually I discovered that a blue insignia on my chest or a red pennant on my lance indicated whose side I was on at that moment. Henry was perfect in every way; he looked just right and when we were charging downhill and other horses were pecking and falling about he was as steady as a rock. He applied his intelligence on these occasions and of course he always had impeccable balance.

Later when we returned from the battle location the close-ups at the castle seemed easy; I even knew whom I was doubling for and could piece together the scenes with the ones we had done before. The hectic battle scenes were done with the second unit

89

but at the castle we were organized by the first assistant and the director's first unit. I always ended up confused by these big films and when I saw the finished article I was still confused!

We did one scene in Tring Park and we were gathered in two armies on top of opposite hills. I was doubling for someone who was obviously the commander of one army — I think it was Peter Finch — and at the signal from the first assistant we charged madly down the hill to clash viciously with the opposing side. I never knew who was doubling for the commander of the other side — he was disguised by a visor, and as none of us had discovered the secret of the blue and red insignia at that time we lashed out at anyone who happened to be near. When I saw the film in later years I could see this scene was obviously wrong, but no-one else I spoke to noticed that English were fighting English and French were fighting French!

I remember someone asking a stunt-man which stunt he thought the most dangerous and he replied: 'Playing dead on the ground while horses ride over you!' This surprised me because to a horseman this did not seem the most dangerous. To me a stunt like being thrown from the castle battlements in full armour into the moat beneath or, as in *Saint Joan*, being burned at the stake, seemed much more dangerous. I remember in *The Black Prince* playing dead several times while the battle raged above me and I never thought the horses would step on me. I had faith in their sensitivity in knowing just where they put all four of their feet!

It is striking how familiarity with a person's features can make you recognise a double immediately on the screen; if you don't know the double well then you *think* you see the star. I knew Jean Seberg's double in *Saint Joan* very well, and when I saw the film I recognized her in the burning scene straight away. In the film where I doubled for Griffith Jones all my friends recognized me immediately and some said it looked as though no attempt had been made to disguise the fact that it was me. The cameramen rely on the psychological angle and I am sure it works. We are conditioned into accepting what we see as the star, unless as I have said we know the features of the double very well.

On *The Black Prince* I had a moment of panic when it was suggested we went to Morocco on location. This was the last thing I wanted because I knew I could not take my horse with me. A friend of mine agreed to go instead of me and a week later his unit sailed off, leaving me behind on the castle lot at MGM. I had just spent a whole day firing arrows from the highest turret when I heard the news . . . My friend had agreed to jump a horse down a slope and the horse had fallen on top of him, breaking my friend's neck. His death in Morocco was a great loss, and we had the job of telling his wife and trying to solve some of the problems. Apparently the stunt had been at the end of the day, the horse was tired and the going rough and my friend, always a daredevil, agreed to do it without preparation.

One of the first things I discovered in this kind of work was that the best stunt-men always spend time sizing up the job and preparing the conditions. I have seen one man actually remove the turf and hide a mattress under it and then in a gallop fall onto that exact spot. Another got 'shot' riding close into camera then fell backwards over the horse in full gallop; but he had prepared safety harness to hold him in position.

Once while galloping downhill in a battle scene I was next to one of the Cossack Riders who broke a leg when his horse fell and rolled on him. These riders gave hair-raising displays all over the country yet in a simple scene galloping downhill this young man sustained serious injury. Unlike my stallion the horses they used were trained to gallop only on the flat while their riders picked up handkerchiefs with their teeth and somersaulted in the saddle. I was always grateful for the schooling my horse had had in the past. The whole programme of his training had developed his intelligence, balance and versatility, making him safe and comfortable to ride under all circumstances.

13

The Circus

An incredible adventure befell us around this time. I was
approached by a small circus company to ride Henry for a
season as one of their star attractions. This was tempting if for
no other reason than that I had never done it before! Neither
had Henry of course, but I felt the medium was right for him. I
had a letter asking me to telephone the writer precisely at
ten-o'-clock the next Monday morning.

'You might as well see what they want!' said Patricia. 'You
haven't a film at the moment and we could manage here.'

'But a season probably means six months!' I argued. I had
already turned down a year's contract for TV work because I
dared not allow myself to be tied down while I had other
short-term jobs; a pity — we should have enjoyed *Robin Hood*!

'Oh, go on — no harm done. Ring them up.'

So I did. A foreign voice answered the telephone. 'Zandizing
Circus,' said the voice, or at least that's what it sounded like.

'You wrote to me about riding in your circus,' I said.

'Ah, yes. Ve would very much like — if you could —'

'Perhaps you could come and see the stallion.'

'Ah, yes. Ve would very much like —'

'Well, then — you say when.'

'Ah, yes. Ve would like — er — to come tomorrow.'

We made the appointment and I hung up.

'Well?' asked Patricia. 'Who are they?'

'Oh, Zingaling — no, Zandizingaling — no . . . Anyway,
they're coming tomorrow.'

I got Henry ready and made a circle in the school with
cavelletti. I had no real idea what I was going to do but thought I
would make it up as I went along. This was often best because

one could sense on some days which movements Henry would do well.

At eleven-o'-clock sharp the next day a car drew up at the stables and we peered out from the tack-room window. A dark Indian-looking man clambered out of the driving side and went round to let his passenger out. This one was equally dark but taller and dressed dramatically in black from head to toe. I'm not sure that they did introduce themselves as Mr Zang and Mr Zing but I will call them this anyway.

'Ve are pleased to meet you.'

They both used the same phrases.

'Yes, ve very much like . . .'

Patricia very politely showed them into the school and they sat, very seriously, on two bales of straw awaiting the display. I asked my head-girl to bring Henry into the yard and I mounted out of sight so that I could make a dramatic entrance into the school. It was all of that. Henry saw the cavelletti and thought I meant him to jump them, which he did — landing us both squarely in the centre of my ring. When he saw the strange gentlemen he started screaming at them at the top of his voice, and then Patricia turned on the music and the loud speaker went peculiar and sounded like a house on fire! However, we regained what composure we had left and started our 'act'. It went well and Henry was in the mood for spectacular movements. I had never known his passage to be better — but I think he was thinking I was going to make him trot over the cavelletti which by necessity were much closer than usual.

After about ten minutes I ended the display and made him take a bow. The dark gentlemen nodded and clapped their hands; not in the way of applause but in the way of summoning a servant.

'Ah — ve think that is very good. Yes, ve very much like.'

'I'm glad,' I said. 'Well — what does the job entail?'

The taller man said it meant my going to places on the South Coast for periods up to three weeks. Most days there would be two performances and before each move a publicity ride through the towns. I told them that a contract for one month at a time would suit me in case I found I could not complete a whole season.

'The season is for six months, this time,' said Zang.

'The season for the winter ve may want you, too!' said Zing.

'But could I have a monthly option?' I insisted.

They weren't happy about this and I could see their point of view. Then I suddenly had a brilliant idea. An old friend, who had ridden for Bertram Mills, could be my stand-in; she had a grey high-school horse and this could take over if I decided I could no longer honour the engagement.

This necessitated taking them to see her 'act', which had to be arranged at a moment's notice in a little paddock belonging to the local pony club. Zang and Zing took it all in their stride and were quite amenable to the idea. The demonstration was very successful and we were able to make an agreement; I was to have a monthly option with my friend as my stand-in if I decided to quit. I was pretty sure I would not last six months but I did want to try.

Then came snag number one.

'Ah, yes — ve would very much like you ride our stallion, too,' said Zang.

'Oh — why is that?' I asked lamely, dreading the worst.

'It is Lipizzaner — but it has only been in circus — it does a few tricks.'

'I'll bet!' I said to myself, then I asked: 'Tricks? What kind of tricks?'

'It does hinds and Spanish Walk and —'

'I'd like to see it first!'

'Ve could arrange for you to ride,' said Zang. 'It is in a stable with its old rider near here!'

'Why does its old rider not ride it in the circus?'

'Oh, very sad. She marry and leave circus.'

It was suggested that the stallion was brought over by box to my stable for me to see and ride in the school. After a telephone call it was arranged more or less straight away but it meant we had to entertain Zang and Zing for lunch. We had barely finished coffee when a huge horse-box arrived with Zangazing Circus emblazoned on the side. The young lady who had ridden the stallion led him out on a head-collar followed by a man who we learned later was her husband. I noticed he hovered about but let his wife do all the handling and at one point when the stallion's rug slipped he took the most elaborate precautions in straightening it. The animal was smaller than Henry and had more Arab quality about him. I liked his looks and he showed a lot of personality but I got the impression that he was not altogether a very happy animal. The young lady tacked him up while her husband held him, I thought, rather reluctantly and Zang and Zing, inscrutable as ever, just stood by and watched.

'Desee will ride him and show you what he can do,' said Zang, then to the girl he said: 'Ve would very much like you to ride him please.'

She got on and rode him cautiously into the school and he spooked at the cavelletti which were still there.

The stallion worked freely but unhappily I thought. The girl cantered him with a flying change and then a rather poor attempt at passage. He also did a full bow and a very good Spanish Walk; but his highlight was the 'hinds'. He went up very high and then walked forward on his hind-legs. Henry's work was more classical and he never did anything as spectacular as this; a Levade was enough strain on his legs and this was all I ever asked from him.

'Would you like to ride him?' asked the girl. She asked me hesitantly as if she did not want to press the point. Zang and Zing obviously wanted me to have a go. I swallowed hard. 'Yes, of course,' I said. 'I'm not sure about the "hinds" though.'

'Just see if he will work for you first,' said the girl's husband.

I sensed something was wrong here but I went into the school and spoke to the horse who responded with ears back, and the girl helped me into the saddle.

They all watched silently as I walked him round. He felt good and gave me a secure feeling — something which Horaya, the Arab stallion, never did; but he hadn't the honesty of Henry. He seemed to resent my commands. We cantered, we attempted passage and we did the Spanish Walk. The girl seemed relieved at my success and was coming forward to my rescue when Zang demanded the 'hinds' movement. Although I was dubious the little stallion had done nothing so far to frighten me so I said: 'Well — all right. What do I do?'

'Hold the strap — pull — and urge him on!'

She raised her hands in front of me and up we went. I clung on like a monkey and we did two or three steps forward. Rearing so high was something I had only done previously with Jackdaw — and I successfully cured him of that!

'Good. Good!' said Zing. 'That was fine.'

We ended the meeting with my agreeing to appear at a coastal resort for the first three-week season and that if their stallion was there and there was no other rider, I would be willing to ride him in one of the 'spectaculars'.

'What a funny thing,' said Patricia afterwards. 'I would have sworn they were frightened of that stallion — all except the girl that is!'

A week later I had a telephone call from an acquaintance nearby who asked: 'Did you have the Zangazing circus people in the other day? I heard you had their stallion over at your place.'

'That's right,' I answered. 'Henry and I are doing a season for them.'

'You didn't ride their stallion, did you?'

'Yes — it's a proper circus horse, that one!'

'It is that! I've known it for some time. The girl exercises it in one of my paddocks. Of course, you do know it doesn't work for men, don't you?'

'Really? Well, it went for me — not very willingly I must admit!'

'You were lucky. Her husband won't go near it — not since it killed a man!'

I was struck dumb. 'Killed a man?' I gasped. She went into the gory details and I realized then why the circus men had treated the stallion so warily. Apparently the groom had gone into the stable to straighten a rug and the horse had turned on him. He was cornered and could not escape. When he was found it looked as if the stallion had savaged him then turned and kicked him to death.

This horrific incident shows how an intelligent horse can react to unfair training. Once the damage has been done the animal can be a danger from then on. How little the animal mind is understood in these cases, and the more intelligent the animal the greater the damage to its emotions.

I rode my three-week season and we had a lot of success. I enjoyed the experience but did not want to go on for the whole six months. We moved to another town and I gave several performances but finally I asked Zang and Zing to release me and let my friend come and take over. She was delighted of course, and before I returned to London we gave two shows as a duel act. Zang was enthusiastic about this and would have liked kept in but I was adamant about leaving.

I escaped riding their stallion only because the girl's husband let her come back to Zangazing for a season and she continued to ride him.

I had thought that my circus stint would have enabled me to have closer contact with Henry, but I found the atmosphere, although a happy one, disturbed me too much for this.

14

The Holiday

We eventually got a well earned holiday. It was during a slack period in August and we decided to take three horses and go off to the New Forest. We chose Henry, Luckystride and Merrylegs. It was a busman's holiday but we knew that if we were not to chase the sun abroad just staying at an English seaside resort would be boring. We could always go into Bournemouth if need be and the horses would give us something to do for part of each day. We stayed at a hotel in Brockenhurst and liveried our horses at a stud-farm nearby. It was great fun for a few days, but we soon decided that a fortnight was too long. Stephen and I went down every morning to prepare the horses and then we rode them back to the hotel to fetch Patricia. The riding was interesting but eventually, owing to the mud, we used the same tracks every day and it got less interesting. As we had quite a bit of sunshine we spent the afternoons on the beaches. As was a custom of mine I always went down to the farm in the evenings to groom and feed the stallion and sometimes this was quite late after dinner . . .

I was alone in the stable one evening and Henry had finished his hay, so I went into the neighbouring barn to find him some more; I always liked to leave him with something to eat. When I returned his stable was empty!

'Henry!' I called. 'Where are you?'

There was utter silence and I peered at the bolt on the door. It was still fastened. The mystery deepened when I searched the place because I could find no hoof-prints and the other horses did not whinney. It was suddenly uncanny. The yard was not an old one, it contained a tack-room and a large barn for fodder and a smaller one for bedding. The gate was shut and the paddock was in fast-deepening shadow. I felt a cold wind gust across my forehead and the leaves on the big oak trees rustled with sudden energy. When an owl screeched I nearly jumped out of my skin.

I almost felt the horse had been spirited away — or he was playing a game with me. 'Henry!' I called again. 'Where are you?' Merrylegs came to the door of her box and peered at me; Lucky was still eating his hay.

I searched the yard again and tested the catch on the gate. Everything was normal and Henry was nowhere to be found. Then just when I was about to give up and call for help, I heard his voice — it was a low-pitched snicker and it came from the barn. I went over and looked in — there was no light but I could make out the white shape of a horse! 'How on earth —' I exploded. He came over and put his nose into my hand. He was munching hay as he looked at me and I swear he was grinning from ear to ear. I led him back to his box and showed him the bolt which he promptly rattled undone, and I took him inside. It was possible the bolt, being loose, had closed itself when he had got out — but he had done it so silently, and how I had missed him in the barn when I was getting the hay I'll never understand.

The highlight of the holiday was the local horse show. We rode down with the idea of relaxing and simply watching it — but Henry caused such a sensation we were asked to give a display. We were announced as the holders of the title for the longest ride in full armour and Henry as England's No.1 film horse! It sounded all right and I must say he looked like a No.1 horse. We had to give an impromptu display using what music was available and I managed to get a number of movements into about fifteen minutes. Everyone was pleased and grateful and I was sure Henry enjoyed every minute of it; one of the musical numbers was the theme from *Limelight*, and for the first time we invented some super slow movements based on the walk, the rein-back and the hock and forehand turns.

On the way back to the hotel we passed a group of gypsies. They were sitting in a picturesque tableau by the side of the road.

One old man came over to speak to me — or rather to Henry.

'Hullo, my beauty!' he said. 'You're a rare breed, aren't you?'

'Lipizzaner,' I offered.

The old man did not look at me but placed his gnarled hand

99

on the stallion's neck. 'Aye. Lipizzaner,' he repeated, and ran his fingers over the brand-mark on the quarters. 'You're an aristocrat of the horse world. My word! You're a wonderful old man!' He then spoke in a foreign tongue.

'Not so old,' I said, but the man ignored me. He was so obviously enjoying his communion with Henry I did not like to interrupt. The other gypsies looked on and smiled.

Suddenly a remarkable thing happened. Whether I gave Henry the aid unconsciously or not I don't know, but I felt him sinking into a bow. I did not check the movement and when he was down in position the old man fondled his head in acceptance. We discovered afterwards that the old man and his family were from the continent and I wondered whether Henry had recognized something in his past.

Henry and I spent a lot of time together and I liked to feel our relationship was absolutely exclusive. We fitted each other very well and to feel part of such a horse was a never-to-be-forgotten feeling. When I discovered things about him I had no part in I felt in some mysterious way an eavesdropper; there should have been no secrets — only deep understanding between us. He was honest with me and it was this complete honesty that mattered most. All human beings keep something back from their fellow kind, whereas he offered everything to me — and if I did not grasp what he offered then surely I had failed him.

We were lucky to see a New Forest mare give birth and to help bring the youngster into the stable. We also had friends down from London to stay as our guests. They stayed one night and in the morning we gave them a ride on Henry and Lucky. It was a bright day and we rode out to a high spot where we changed horses so that our friends could ride back. Stephen rode both ways on Merry and as Patricia and I drove back in the car the heavens opened — I had never seen it rain so much! We waited at the hotel for our friends to appear, and in the distance I saw Henry cantering with his head down between his legs and the other two in hot pursuit. Henry was furious because the rain beat straight into his face and it was a heavy penetrating rain.

We were both laughing and our friends, who were not prepared for such a soaking, had to join in the merriment — although I suspected they were not entirely amused. We let them escape for a hot bath while we rubbed and dried the horses down. Henry was still peeved when I went in to change his rug

100

later that evening. His long damp mane had curled over his neck and his sleek quarters were dull and wispy. 'I'll make you look your old self tomorrow,' I whispered. 'Come on — cheer up — return journey. It had been suggested we call in to see friends

He could not have understood my facetious remark, but as he looked at me with his ears flicking backwards and forwards it did look as if he was trying to!

We spent a day at the place where they held the sales of ponies — and we were taken back to the time we had spent there years ago when we had all gone a bit crazy and bought some highly unsuitable young-stock. Once one gets the bug there is no stopping at a sale — everything looks worth bidding for!

The holiday ended and we loaded the horses up for our return journey. It had been suggested we call in to see friends on the way and at the time it seemed a good idea. The trouble was we lost our way and got caught in a flood.

We found ourselves in a dark lane overhung with trees. A swollen river running alongside had burst its banks and flooded the roadway. We drove slowly through the water but it was deeper than we thought and suddenly we were at a standstill — unable to move. I got out of the Land-Rover and found myself up to my thighs in water. Cursing, I waded onto dry land and looked round for the nearest house. I could see a bungalow across a field and yelled to the others that I would go over for help. The horses whinnied and Henry gave a loud scream.

'It's all right!' I called. 'Don't worry . . .'

The bungalow was deserted but I suddenly saw a face peering at me from the bottom of the garden. 'Can you help?' I asked. 'We've broken down just outside here. Is there a garage or a farm nearby?' The face became a head and the head became a body — and I was confronted by a wizened old woman. 'I'm hard of hearing. Speak up will you!' she rasped.

'I've broken down!' I shouted.

'You've got stuck in them floods — you silly fool — couldn't you see them?'

'How was I to know the road dipped just there!'

'Eh? Speak up!'

'Can you tell me if there is —'

'A garage you say? No, there isn't! But my son will get you out.'

Her son was only too willing — at a fee — and was soon seen

racing over the fields complete with ropes draped round his neck. I had no alternative but to agree to his help — and his fee!

'I suppose you do this often?' I said.

'Oh yes,' he said, not without a twinkle in his eye. 'It happens every day at this time o' year.'

He pulled us out with an ancient tractor and both he and I were soaked to our skins. The difference was that he was in the tattiest of old jeans and I was in my newest Simpson's cavalry twills. We had to get the plugs dried out and I rang our friends who very kindly drove out to help. We did manage to have a drink with them and then together we got the engine started and began our belated journey home.

We sang to keep up our spirits and Henry must have thought we were all off our heads; he joined us once or twice but it sounded more like remonstrance than harmony. It reminded me of a time coming out from the White City when we had been loaded with Arab horses. The traffic was thick and fast and we all wore fancy hats left over from some gymkhana — and we burst into song, raised our arms to halt the traffic and drove straight out into it with determination. The traffic had to screech to a stop in all directions and we waved in acknowledgment and amidst swearing drivers drove off towards Shepherd's Bush.

15

The Burglar

Henry was of course a remarkable horse . . . One can do or think a thing automatically for years, until one day one starts to think deeply for the first time — and the real truth begins to dawn. An incident now to be related proves the point and probably took me nearer to understanding the mentality of my stallion than anything else.

As I have mentioned earlier Henry could, if he wished, unbolt doors and let himself out of his box. He did this by grasping the bolt in his mouth, fiddling with it until it gave way and then by rattling his door he could slip the bottom bolt also. Bottom bolts tend to get neglected and weakened by strain, and it was usually an old bolt he could rattle undone. Our stable was an old one and some of the bolts were not all that secure. But in his own yard Henry had never tried to let himself out — except this once!

I was away on a film and Patricia was visiting a friend; Stephen was at school and the staff had all gone home at seven-o'-clock. The horses were alone for about two hours, and like all good burglars the young man who now appeared had made it his job to know the place was empty.

Our tack-room was secure with Ingersoll locks, but the office complete with silver trophies was not, nor of course the stable with the day-rugs hanging on pegs at the end of each row. It was a simple thing to climb over the big gate into the yard and, once inside, to have the complete run of the place. There was one dog somewhere but he had been accidentally shut in with Henry. The horses were accustomed to hear people about the place and there was nothing to arouse their suspicion nor that of the dog.

The burglar filled a sack with things from the office, and then he went off to collect the beautiful red and gold day-rugs from the boxes. This is where an odd thing happened. He had collected some of them and then passed the stallion's box; Henry looked at him and obviously did not get the right vibrations. At this time the dog might well have barked, which would have given the horse the feeling that something was wrong.

The man took down the last rug and turned to leave, and at the same time Henry unbolted his door. The man left the stable-block and walked towards the yard; he heard Henry rattling his door but thought nothing of it. It wasn't until he felt the hot breath of the stallion down his neck that he realized something had happened; he turned a frightened face to Henry, dropped the rugs and foolishly started to run. Henry loved to feel free and he gave joyous little rears, which to the uninitiated were frightening. The man was terrified, and to add to his troubles the bulldog Gillie thought: what fun! — and joined in the chase.

The man was cornered in the yard and cut off from any possible retreat. On one side was a coach-house, on the other a stable-block, and beyond was the main gate. Henry stood his ground and played a sort of cat and mouse game and Gillie kept snapping at the man's heels. The odd thing was that the stallion kept the man there until Patricia came back and opened up the stables. By the time he was rescued he was a bundle of nerves and only too willing when the police arrived to be taken to jail.

As soon as Patricia unlocked the big gate to enter the yard Henry whinnied once loudly, as if he was warning her that things were not quite right. When she came round the corner and saw the burglar cowering against a wall with his hands over his head Henry stood rock-still, as if waiting for her command. Fortunately she had a friend with her who rang for the police and she just grasped the stallion by the forelock and waited for help. Henry acknowledged her by rubbing his head on her shoulder and the bulldog came and sat at her feet.

'I'm sorry, missus,' stammered the man. 'I thought he was going to kill me!'

Patricia stopped herself saying: 'He would never do that,' and answered instead: 'He would have done if I hadn't returned when I did!'

Henry allowed Patricia to put him back in his box and as the police left the yard with the burglar he gave an almighty scream.

When he heard it the young man went limp at the knees and practically had to be carried out to the car.

Henry's apprehension of the burglar was an incredible feat. If he was helped by Gillie, who would never have done such a thing on his own, it is still incredible. The local press reported the incident but I don't think many people believed it. I swear that the above account is absolutely true.

Soon after this we had invitations to take horses down to the sea. We had a coastal flat near Worthing at the time and had made the acquaintance of the owners of an Arab stud farm nearby. It was something I had always wanted to do with Henry — to ride him in the sea.

Years previously, long before I met Henry, I had spent six months in Yorkshire helping a friend run a hunting stable and we had always exercised on the beaches between Filey and Flamboro Head. It was very exciting, and I remember on one occasion getting cut off by the tide and reaching our cliff-path just when the sea had reached our saddles and it looked like swimming for it. We had fun too with concrete tank-traps through which we could only gallop by putting our legs up round the horses' necks. I was caught up by a Butlin holiday camp whilst there and spent six months as a Red Coat — teaching the campers to ride! We hired thirty horses which we kept in fields and every day we caught twenty (usually the same twenty) and took the campers out in long strings on the cliff-tops. Today this would be known as Pony Trekking. I took the campers on the beach only once; the whole twenty horses took off and half galloped into the sea, where the riders fell off, and the other half disappeared flat out for Flamboro Head!

The whole thing had been an extraordinary and highly enjoyable experience. I was introduced on the stage every week with the other Red Coats so that the new intake of campers knew who we were and what we taught. Eric Robinson was the orchestra conductor at the time and he always played 'A-hunting we will go!' when I appeared.

Sometimes I would ride alone on the beaches. I could hear the bell boom at Filey Brig and the misty cliffs of Flamboro seemed a long way ahead. There was a vastness about everything that dwarfed me, making me feel an infinitesimal part of the whole . . .

Riding at Worthing was not the same — but Henry didn't

105

know the difference and we enjoyed the experience very much. He liked to stand and splash the water up into my face, and when we cantered he shook his head as the salt-spray stung his nostrils. Once again we were able to give a riding display for a local horse show. This was a show organized by our friends and the proceeds went to charity. We arrived there on foot as the stable was only a mile away and Henry screamed madly at the attendants on the gate. He must have been in a very stallionish mood that day because he greeted both man and horse with a great deal of voice and leg-striking. 'Behave yourself!' I scolded, and he answered me with a loud whinny.

Our exhibition was successful but I had a lot of difficulty making the stallion behave; he wanted to clown everything, and all the movements I asked him to do he exaggerated or changed into something else. He made me laugh, but I soon became red in the face with embarrassment in case people realized things weren't going exactly as they should! In one movement I usually gave a progressive volte followed by a half-pass changing the volte movements into half-passes from the centre line. This looked quite good and was a simple routine for Henry but he mucked it up completely. He cantered the last volte and made the passes look like a bending-race! When it came to cantering he jumped and turned like an acrobat every time I asked for a change of leg. I knew he was enjoying himself by the way he cantered into the changes with a tossing down of the head and a strangled whinny coming from his throat.

I was glad our friends were not dressage enthusiasts because they would have been horrified by Henry's performance. He would sometimes give a very good display, but he had to be shut in a Covered School without distractions before he would give a perfect one. But it really didn't matter; at least the display showed off his personality and his movements were brilliant. People watching were smiling and our ovation was one of the best we had ever had. What made me mad was the fact that Henry had given his own performance without even listening to me — and it had still been a great success.

'What fun he is!' said our friends. 'Such a personality! He really is a joy to watch!'

'Yes,' I answered — and Henry snickered.

We rode him several times in the sea and he played with the waves and the spray like a child. One day there were some donkeys being ridden along the sands and it was the funniest thing to see Henry invite them to play. 'They don't want you!' I told him. Actually they did — because they brought their unwilling riders over to see us. Henry wasn't too sure and sniffed at them suspiciously, then splashed them and screamed vigorously. The donkeys brayed. That floored him and for a moment he was nonplussed — then he resumed his antics in the water. The donkeys loved it and showed a lot of interest; but finally their riders were able to persuade them to resume their journey and Henry watched them go with wide eyes and the little strangled noise coming from his throat.

One other incident on this holiday worth recording was Henry's reaction to our fibreglass rowing boat. We would take it out when the tide was coming in, so the water was seldom more than three foot deep. One day I was in the boat with Stephen and Patricia was riding Henry. I threw her a rope that was fixed in the boat to the anchor and she, for fun, gave the end of it to Henry. He took it in his mouth and actually towed me for about half a mile in the shallow water. He did the pulling as my wife sat on him doing nothing.

Yes, Henry enjoyed the sea. We enjoyed it ourselves. Henry was more tuned to our feelings and reactions than we ever realized.

16

Advertising — and *Saint Joan*

Life was good. Henry was part of it and although other animals came and went we felt he would go on forever. A horse's life is a short one — and a dog's life even shorter; they stay with you for a while, grow part of you and then they have to leave you. It is sad but it is part of the pattern of life and must be accepted. We lost the bulldog, Gillie, and we inherited a poodle called Ba-Ba. We bought this little white dog as a companion for my mother-in-law when her husband died, and no animal could have been more successful. Ba-Ba stayed with her mistress through everything, went on holidays with her, guarded her at night, attacked a burglar; and when her mistress was dying of cancer stayed outside the bedroom door until the end.

I felt very sorry for this little dog because she had allowed herself to become so close to her mistress. When we took her over, she was 'lost' for weeks; you would see her just sitting, big eyes fixed on a window or a door — waiting for something or someone she felt she should remember! Eventually she 'adopted' my wife and things were better for her; she would keep so close to Patricia she never needed a lead — wherever my wife was, Ba-Ba was a foot behind. It was pathetic and very sweet. We soon discovered how intelligent she was: she did all the dog-training routines without ever being taught.

We let her have a litter of puppies and after finding homes for the rest we kept one little bitch. We called her Bumpi. She was entirely different from her mother; a delightfully independent little scatterbrain. Of course we adored Bumpi, and I must confess her personality outshone even her mother's. She very soon established that she was top-dog too and poor old Ba-Ba had to take a back seat.

Naturally these dogs were friends of Henry, and once again

108

photographs were taken for greeting cards and advertisements. Ba-Ba would sit on Henry's back looking angelic and Bumpi would sit unwillingly between his forelegs or some such place. They made a pretty picture and Henry tolerated the little dogs very well. Now the colour scheme was complete — except for white cats; I was superstitious about those! — for we had horses, ponies and dogs whiter than white! It did not take long before the group was asked to advertise all kinds of things from washing powder to cocktails.

One of the funniest jobs was for a large cigarette firm. The advertising executive rang me and discussed the possibility. He had no experience with animals but it had been suggested by his managing director that they used our horses and poodles in their next campaign. I agreed to an interview at the stables and all the animals were groomed and turned out in their red and gold rugs; even Ba-Ba and Bumpi had little coats to match.

The executive arrived in an Aston Martin car with his girl-friend dripping in mink and diamonds sitting beside him. Such an un-horsey pair you couldn't wish to see!

'We've come to see the white animals,' he said. 'We have an appointment.' He was addressing me but obviously thought I was just the groom.

'I see,' I answered. 'I'll go and find out if they're in!'

I went into the tack-room and told the staff they had arrived. We all watched them timidly approach the ponies and the girl-friend poked a nervous finger into Muffin's face. Nothing irritated the pony more than this, so he promptly took a bite — and it made the girl scream. The man then turned, tripped over a wheel-barrow and upset a bucket of water. At that moment I let the poodles out and they ran yapping excitedly across the yard, which made the young lady scream again in terror. I took a deep breath and returned to them; when I said I was the owner they both looked at me with distrust.

'Call off your beastly little dogs!' wailed the young lady.

'Your pony bit Fiona!' complained the man.

I apologized and did eventually show them some of the ponies being lunged free in the school and Henry with the poodles on his back. They were impressed but so nervous of the animals that the whole thing was impossible.

'What would they have to do?' I asked.

'Well . . .' said the man, slowly. 'I thought we could use them in various famous places — you know, St Paul's Cathedral, Tower of London, the Tate Gallery . . .'

'What — just loose?' I ventured.

'Yes — and then in the foreground we would have models smoking our cigarettes.'

I had visions of Henry and the ponies running amok in the Tate Gallery and smiled. 'I'm not sure that would work out,' I said.

'It sounds a marvellous idea,' said the young lady.

'Couldn't you have them in famous places like Cheddar Gorge, Brands Hatch or Wimbledon Common?' I suggested desperately.

The man thought this might be possible but they had thought in terms of famous buildings really . . . The outcome was that they would 'let us know' and, somewhat relieved, I guided them out of the yard and safely back into their Aston Martin car. After this we did a very good tobacco advertisement. We used the yard with a man smoking in the foreground and all the horses, poodles and white doves in the background; I never knew if our un-horsey cigarette pair ever saw it.

I was still doing film work but the stable took up more and more of my time. I gave lessons and took classes every day and like most instructors found myself forever in the covered school — with less and less time to ride myself. Nothing kills incentives faster than teaching; painters who teach lose originality, pianists who teach lose their ability to play — and riding instructors lose the incentive to train or compete! I gave exhibitions, I judged at shows, I had the occasional film work, but I never had the real time to dedicate myself to schooling and 'creating'. I had become commercialized.

That is why we loved our flat on the coast — it gave us a complete change and peace . . . Before it was too late we knew we had to change our way of life. We wanted to buy a stable with land in the country, take our mares and our stallions and give them a fuller and more natural environment. I suppose all successful businesses have to become commercialized in the end, but I had a growing feeling I wanted to escape back into the beginning! The beginning is youth and youth is happiness — and I knew I owed it to Henry, to give him the time and tolerance that he willingly gave to me.

So the search was on; not very consistently because we went

down to the coast so seldom and our free time got less and less. But the seed was sown and we knew that one day it would develop into what we wanted . . .

The film work, when it came, kept me busy and on call for sometimes as long as three months at a time. For *The Moonrakers* I went on location to Corfe and we had one memorable shot to do on the top of Portland Bill. The cameras were set up on the cliff top about half a mile away and the location unit had gathered on a farm nearby. The horse-boxes had arrived and the master-of-the-horse was busy preparing them for the day's shooting. Having driven down with a friend I did not hurry and wasted time having coffee with the catering staff, not realizing that the actual location was still half a mile off. We went down to mount our horses much too late and my friend looked round for his horse and discovered that someone else had taken it. The only one left on the lines was a big bay with a very wild eye.

'You'll have to have that one,' I told him. The groom said nothing but I noticed a grim smile on his face. My friend mounted.

'Hurry up! They've been gone for ages and they're shooting at nine-thirty!' shouted someone.

We rode off at a fair pace and the big bay pulled on rather alarmingly. 'How is he?' I asked.

'Bloody strong!' said my friend. 'I think the other boys knew a thing or two when they left this one behind!'

I realized suddenly we had been conned. Some of the riders had been at Corfe the previous day and had learned the ropes; it was pretty obvious this horse had been left on the lines because he was a bit of a rogue! We had nearly reached the location when the big bay gave an enormous leap forward and my friend went flat out towards the set-up on the edge of the cliff. As the big horse shot amongst them cameramen scattered and horses turned in panic. No-one said anything — and this only proved what I thought; even the assistants only raised an eyebrow and made few remarks.

When I saw the scene we were to do I realized why no-one had wanted the big mad bay. We were to gallop round a corn-field on the very edge of a sheer drop to the sea. I could see sailing boats glinting on the water like match-box toys and great big

111

jagged rocks washed by foaming waves. It was not like any of us to complain about our horses so my friend accepted the inevitable and we rode up through the corn-field for the first take.

It was hair-raising. George Baker was the star and I cannot remember who doubled for him now. He did most of his own riding but of course this scene was too hazardous for him. He kept vaulting onto his horse — and after several days he complained of pains in his chest. 'The way you vault on I should think you have cracked all your ribs!' I said, and sure enough he had! He was in agony for three weeks.

The first shot on the cliff was downhill then round a bend. It was terrifying, and my friend had difficulty in keeping the big bay from passing us all and scattering the cameras. He did this by facing the animal into our tails. The trouble was that each time we did the shot the bay got more and more excited until he was leaping forward and landing on top of the horse in front! We were laughing about it but knew the dangers. I finally said to one of the assistants: 'You do realize that horse will leap over the cliff eventually, don't you?'

He grinned as we passed but said nothing. The next time we did the scene the horse leapt so madly he let one leg slip over the edge of the cliff. The assistant had taken note, however, and before we did the scene again he came over to us and said: 'I think you had better have another horse.'

'Pleasure!' answered my friend.

Another one was found and the big bay ridden back to the lines by one of the boys. Henry called after the bay and the animal answered. Perhaps he had lost a friend . . . but at least I had not!

I was asked by my agent to attend an audition for the part of the third soldier in *Saint Joan*, a film being made by Otto Preminger. I was sure this was a formality as I hated auditions and the job, I thought, was a foregone conclusion. I was called soon after this and reported to Shepperton Studios on the first day of shooting. It was a big production and Jean Seberg, straight from drama school and repertory, was a young girl doomed to instant stardom. Otto Preminger had chosen her for the part of Joan and was determined to make her the best actress for the role. Physically she looked the part, but I personally never thought she captured the feeling for the character. She couldn't ride very well but she had my old horse Jackdaw and he carried her all through the picture without once putting a foot wrong. He always seemed to sense when a rider was a beginner, much to my surprise — having known him when he was a very headstrong young horse. I had sold him before Henry came on the scene for the film *Knights of the Round Table*, and when MGM sold the horses I was advised to buy him back. They said they would always hire him from me, he did the job so well; but I let someone else buy him who specialized in film horses — and met the horse on every horsey film from then on!

That first day on *Saint Joan* we used someone else's horses and we had difficult scenes to do indoors. There was very little room, and one of my fellow soldiers was a young actor who had only ridden for a few months. Every time we saw action the horses kept trying to whip round. The young actor could not keep his horse facing into camera and I sensed Preminger was getting angry . . .

Suddenly he screamed: 'Get these horses out of here! I want some good ones that can stand still!'

Everybody was terrified of Otto and there was a great deal of panic. I didn't know him at this stage and wondered why everyone was getting into such a state. The outcome was a change in schedule for the day and the horses were packed off from whence they came.

This was where Henry came into his own and on the next day the scenes were filmed much more calmly. But by the fourth take I was as nervous of Preminger as everybody else. The young actor said his one line and I thought he did very well but Preminger yelled at him: 'You are not to look at the camera! I saw you looking at the camera!'

The episode embarrassed us all and I dreaded making a mistake in case Preminger raved at me also. I just missed having this happen on one occasion when after a coffee break I had to return to the scene which was one in a yard with three of us grooming our horses. For the sake of continuity I went across the lighted stage to retrieve the brushes I had been using. Otto saw me and was just about to yell: 'What is that man doing walking across there!' when the continuity-girl, realizing what I was doing, managed to stop him. I thought my embarrassing moment had come and my heart had already missed a beat!

When we had finished the studio shots we went on location and that was much more enjoyable; we returned indoors for the burning scenes of course but these were without our horses. Jean Seberg used to pop in to see us when arriving at the studio in the mornings and we often all had coffee in the canteen. We liked her before the make-up boys had gone over her because she was then completely natural. When talking to her I always felt she was unable fully to grasp the enormous opportunity her part in *Saint Joan* was giving her. She seemed very young and often talked of marriage, and showed a lot of interest in the fact that her 'three soldiers' were married men with young families. I have often read about her in the newspapers since but she never appeared to become as big a star as we thought she would.

Although she grew very fond of Jackdaw Jean was not particularly horsey-minded. I often wish I had shown her what Henry could do but the opportunity to show him off never came on this picture. On location we had to follow Jean everywhere and the riding was normal and straightforward. I had to grow a rough beard, but on the first occasion I wore a false one and Henry took one look at it and took it off with his teeth. I had a horrible feeling that when Otto demanded action he would see me regaining it from Henry's mouth . . . Luckily I had regained my beard and my composure before this happened.

While I was working on *Saint Joan* the BBC asked me to give six two-minute talks on riding. It fitted in all right because although I was on call to the studios I only had to go two or three days each week. I found two minutes far too short but it fitted into a sporty slot, apparently, in another programme. I divided my six parts into Trot, Canter, Dressage, Showing, Hunting and Jumping and Patricia thought it quite remarkable that my pupils advanced so rapidly in such a short time! The producer said he would probably call on me for a TV programme one day — but after quite a long time I am still waiting! I often criticize riding programmes on TV, but if people have to cover so much ground and complete their series on a tight time schedule no wonder they come over somewhat clipped.

After several weeks on location, including the raft scenes on Frensham Ponds, we returned to the studio. I had the doubtful pleasure of eating at the same table as Otto Preminger and was fascinated by the way in which he shovelled food into his mouth. On this occasion Diana Dors, working on another sound stage, was in the canteen as well and I was surprised to find her more petite than I had imagined. She was still in heavy make-up and was, unfortunately, wearing the most ill-fitting and unglamorous trouser-suit I have ever seen. Years previously I remembered seeing Vivien Leigh in this same canteen looking every inch a film-star and very beautiful.

We attended the burning scene and it was the biggest crowd call of all. A wonderful set was built and the wood was piled high around the stake. Although I had to lead Henry through once I never saw the shot in the finished film. As I have previously said I knew Jean's double well and while the scene was being completed we three soldiers were merely standing in the crowd as spectators. A fire like this is usually done with portable gas-pipes under the faggots and when the director shouts Action the gas is lit and flares up realistically and then dies down again when the order to Cut is given. The wood in this scene was treated but a lot of it did catch alight. On these occasions there is always a fire unit on hand so it is safe enough.

Otto Preminger bullied Jean Seberg before she performed, deliberately making her cry — and when he wanted more realism he put her up at the stake herself. This was not a publicity stunt although the papers reported it as if it were. Jean was terrified and when Otto shouted Cut, the fire went out but a lot of it remained. He was not the only one who helped snatch Miss Seberg from the flames!

Strangely enough, when we left the sound stage on the last day with the smell of fire in our nostrils we emerged to find the studio lot covered with snow. Henry found it all most amusing. He played with it, took mouthfuls and blew them into my face. I tried to mount him but before I could do so he went down and rolled in the snow. 'Get up you silly great idiot!' I shouted. But he was enjoying it so much I started to laugh.

'He'll break the saddle,' said someone. 'Get the silly great bastard up!'

I tried to pull him up but at that moment the girth broke and his saddle slipped off. 'Grab it!' I said. 'Before he rolls on it!' Too late. He flattened my beautiful sheepskin saddle and then remained on his back with his legs in the air for what seemed an

115

eternity. I am sure he was wriggling about because he liked the cold crunchiness on his back.

'Henry,' I scolded. 'This has gone far enough! Get up!!' Much to my surprise he did, but just when I started to lead him off he went down again. By this time everybody was laughing at him and I began to think their laughter was making him do it all the more; he did so love playing to the gallery. When he did finally decide to give it up I snowballed him and he then tried to catch them in his mouth. It was the first and last time I played with him in the snow. He had of course seen weather like this before but that had been when we were riding in Richmond Park — on this occasion at Shepperton I was leading him in hand and he always made this an excuse to play up.

Talking of Richmond Park, I had to give William Franklyn riding lessons at this time for a film he was making. I read the script and worked out a series of lessons to include the sort of things he would have to do. This meant riding in the Park and trotting and cantering in various directions with the reins in the left hand, leaving the sword hand free. A mutual friend, who was a great success in the Brian Rix farces, accompanied him. This friend was a naturally funny person and like a lot of funny people did not like being laughed at. We started off badly because their car, the Rolls Royce once belonging to Sir Alexander Korda, broke down and I had to rescue them six miles from the stables. We did eventually get them both onto their horses and started up the road. Then a woman pushing a pram appeared suddenly and as we passed, her baby threw a teddy bear into the street. Henry looked at the toy disdainfully and Bill's friend, being the perfect gentleman, jumped off his horse to pick it up.

'Oh thank you —' said the woman gratefully.

Friend Toby mounted his horse again awkwardly and promptly fell off it on the other side! He was very tall and the horse wasn't very big. I got him on again and we proceeded to Richmond Park.

This was one of many lessons and each time I dreaded arriving at the Park because the two found the ancient place so full of medieval atmosphere that instead of listening to me they would both go into raptures about the wonderful old trees and the feeling of past history. As Bill had to ride with one

116

hand he let his horse wander all over the place and I had difficulty in persuading him to do what I wanted. Bill and Toby were great fun — and I never go into Richmond Park now without thinking about them!

17

The Animal Mind

We had known Vera Cody for many years and admired her work. When we first met her she had her High School horse Goldie. This horse had performed in variety theatres all over England; Max Bygraves had used him at the London Palladium and exhibitions by Vera were the highlights of many a horse show or riding-club competition. Vera had a craze at one time to collect skewbald horses and we found her several; I think she ran a riding school at this time with her friend Marjorie, but this was soon abandoned and the skewbalds sold.

These two widowed ladies had an incredible way with animals and for this reason I found them two of the most interesting people I had ever met. Certainly Vera was then one of the leading High School riders in the country and still is, because at the time of writing I am pleased to discover she has found another horse to school! I always felt Henry had an affinity with Goldie — and one day Vera came to our yard when he was being ridden; naturally she fell for him and would have loved to buy him. She offered me what was then a huge sum of money but to me Henry, of all the horses I had had before or since, was beyond price. If I had known Vera as well then as I do now I would have let her ride him in exhibition but my wife and I kept him to ourselves — even our staff only rode him occasionally.

It is a strange thing to say but when Henry had gone in later years Vera and Marj seemed to be involved in him far more. Their love for him, and indeed for all animals, was a revelation even for me. When Vera lost Goldie it made me feel the two horses were inextricably moulded into one. To visit the home of these two ladies was an education, and it was the start of knowledge that took me closer to understanding the mind of Henry.

Marj would ask us to supper and we would watch badgers, foxes and wild cats eating together on the lawn. Vera would show us Goldie doing tricks in his paddock with her giving commands from her kitchen window and the two would show us their pet foxes and their talking parrots.

Vera collected paintings and old prints of horses and she could never resist buying whenever she saw one she liked. The trouble was Marj didn't like hundreds of pictures on every conceivable bit of wall-space, so Vera would hang a selection and change them every day. I used to love to go to her house and ask to see the new paintings. She would take me to her bedroom and we spent ages pulling the pictures from under the bed and admiring them. Today she collects driving-prints because her new horse actually does High School while she drives him from her trap!

It was Vera and Marj's attachment to animals that made me realize we had never spent enough time with the stallion to develop his understanding. As I have said, I had often thought that if one could live as closely with a horse as one does with a dog, one would discover much more intelligence in the animal. Here was the proof. Vera had lived closely with her horse, both at home and in circus, as close as it was possible for anyone to get, and Goldie had learned to understand and anticipate her thoughts.

Goldie was a well-bred Palomino gelding, but Vera always said she felt Henry had more intelligence. Vera had the uncanny ability to know what she could make her horse do. If she said 'He will do piaffe', he eventually did; if she said 'He will lie down', he did; and so on. She showed me what complete dedication could achieve. It is not sufficient to *say* you will school your horse to do something if you don't absolutely believe he will do it. She didn't believe — she knew.

I saw this working every time I watched Vera riding Goldie, and I realized I would perhaps come a little way to this understanding but I knew I would never be capable of going the whole way. I think Vera would have enjoyed a more complete one-ness with Henry than I did; and I regret not letting her try. Henry offered all this to me but I was incapable of receiving it; too many distractions, too much contact with my other horses, it was an incomplete closeness. I needed to prove that he could attune himself to me, and I knew my way of life prevented it.

119

The animal mind has always intrigued me. The reason we love animals is because of the innocent trust they give us. Innocence is a purity, and when they show trust then they cannot understand the vices that are in us; we feel we cannot damage that trust by letting them see our baser selves — so the result is love.

The reason people do not understand the animal mind is simply that they are unable to break the barriers. There are barriers, both biological and psychological, between humans and animals, as there are barriers also between the species — bovine, equine, canine, feline, and so on. We can place cows and horses in a field together and they tolerate each other but they cannot totally integrate. The dog and the cat keep the barrier and do not cross it, but of course experiments show a closeness can be created and a trust built up between the species, some kind of mutual tolerance and attunement to each other's thoughts and actions. This is what I feel some people have with their dog or their cat — but seldom with their horses; the fundamentals are difficult and there are insurmountable divisions. But with Vera and Marj the miracle had happened and they were closer to their horses than anyone I knew.

The amusing period when I tried to drive Henry must be related. As I have said, he would long-rein beautifully and I knew he had the temperament to be driven. Vera was very keen on driving and possessed a magnificent selection of vehicles whereas I had never had anything more glamorous than a dog-cart. Up until then we had always kept a cob or two to use if a driving job came our way; one I remember was a Highland mare called Mollie. I saw her in a field with the longest winter coat possible and thought she would make an ideal driving pony, a bit common, but that didn't matter. I bought her cheaply; the owners obviously thought she was an ordinary little cob too — which is not what she turned out to be.

'What shall we do with her — she has a coat about three inches long!' I said. I had felt her legs but the hair and feather were too thick to give a true picture.

'Let's clip her right out,' said my head-girl.

This was decided so I went off and left her to it. Imagine my surprise when I saw the little mare again and didn't recognize her! She had clipped out beautifully, her legs were fine and her face was dished. I immediately realized we had something

120

special here — not the common cob I had thought. We made efforts to find out about her breeding and it transpired she was a registered Highland mare with dozens of prizes in-hand! Henry adored this mare and I must say that once she was clipped out she looked a most attractive companion for him. I liked driving her because she was steady and willing. Henry was often ridden by the side of her when she was in the dog-cart. It made a pretty picture. It was because of this I decided to make them change roles and put the stallion in the trap.

He took the harness very well and we had no problem getting him between the shafts. I walked about with him and he was as steady as a rock; he looked back at the trap once or twice but he was obviously not afraid of it. 'I think he will take to it very well,' I called to Patricia. 'It would look good on TV — perhaps we could borrow one of Vera's glamorous traps!'

Patricia came down to the front gate of the stable to see him and, like a fool, I stepped back beside her to admire the combination. 'Don't they look gorgeous together —' I started, when Henry took one sly look at me and trotted off down the lane. 'Hi! Henry — stop!' I yelled and started to run after him. The faster I ran the faster he trotted. We went down the lane into the road, turned sharp right through someone's unfenced rhododendron bushes, into a private drive past the front door of a neighbour's house — then finally an about turn into the local Golf Club. This was the end! I had visions of him ploughing up the greens and overturning the trap into a bunker.

I was sure Henry was enjoying every minute; he probably thought the trap was some form of long-reining by remote control. He was quite unconcerned about the trap and judged his distances beautifully. The farce went on with golfers looking on in amazement and one or two raising a menacing club. All this made very little difference to Henry, who trotted with elegance, cadence and joy past the terraces and out onto the broad green towards No.2 hole. I ran round the back of the club-house, being much too self-conscious to be seen, which made it seem even more incongruous.

'I do believe there is no-one in that trap!' said one man.

'Perhaps one of the honourable members is using the horse as a caddie,' said another.

The outcome was that I was joined by half a dozen golfers and we all trotted in an exhausted straggle after Henry. As if he knew the game had gone on long enough, he suddenly swung round and started making for home. This meant coming back past the club-house again and as the stallion approached his pursuers they all turned chicken and didn't dare make a grab. I could have done so but as the others turned, falling over themselves in my direction, I tripped and took an undignified header over an ornamental pot.

The episode was causing some considerable concern by this time and I prayed that my stable-staff had found their way to the golf course. They had — but they had entered by a different gate, so Henry continued on his unmolested way out onto the road. I was intensely embarrassed to see him promptly go down the same private drive, past the neighbour's house (this time with everyone standing at the front door!), out again by the other gate, through the unfenced rhododendron bushes, and lo and behold — perverse devil — back up our lane to the stables.

'Been for a nice run?' asked Patricia sweetly, standing at Henry's head. I was too winded to answer — and Henry wasn't even breathing heavily. 'He's a swine!' I muttered. It took me some while to live this down. Most neighbours thought Henry and I were a pair of eccentrics anyway — and incidents like this helped to prove how right they were. Vera and Marj never stopped laughing. I gave up the idea of borrowing a glamorous trap and when advertising jobs turned up I stuck to Mollie in the dog-cart.

18

Breaking the Barriers

It was strange how circumstances gave me the chance to test my theories. A friend was keen to make a film about a stallion living free in natural surroundings and he approached me with his ideas. As we discussed the possibility I realized that if I could do this job I would be able, at last, to live close enough to Henry to try and plumb the depths of his intelligence. My friend had the support of a rich backer and I agreed to meet them at his flat in London to finalize the contract.

I seldom went to London — I was not happy with the bustle and the one-way streets. I managed to make my way to the address my friend Joe had given me. It was just off Marble Arch and looked decidedly wealthy. I went up in the lift and found the flat I wanted and rang the bell. Voices were raised inside and then a maid opened the door. I mentioned my name.

'Madam, you expects,' she said and walked off down a long passageway, at the end of which she opened a pair of stained-glass doors and I was shown into an ostentatious room with high ceilings.

'Please to sit,' said the maid, and left me. I was beginning to think I had come to the wrong flat (especially as there was a pair of lady's tights on a chair!) when Joe entered from an adjoining room. 'Hullo — I'm so pleased you could come,' he said. 'I will introduce you to Mrs Jill Owenska.'

'Who is Jill Owenska?' I asked.

'The backer for my film — I told you —' he whispered.

I nodded. 'A woman?'

'Yes — didn't I say?' Joe seemed a trifle nervous and he poured me a drink. He must have known I drank very little but I thought I would be polite and take it.

A moment later Mrs Owenska came into the room. She was a

very striking woman in her forties and dressed in a flowing sort of day-gown. She looked theatrical and later I learned she had been an actress, but now she was a wealthy widow who liked to put her money into films. We got along very well. She had ridden ponies as a girl, loved horses and was longing to meet my wonderful stallion. Joe had a hard time pinning her down to business but eventually we agreed to work with all expenses paid and take a percentage of the profits when the film was released. This gave us both a free hand to do whatever we liked; Joe was to arrange the camera-crews and the locations and I was to arrange the set-ups the script demanded. We could employ whom we liked and all hotels and incidentals were to be met by Mrs Owenska.

On the face of it it sounded all right, but actually although we never lost money on the venture we never made any either. The film was completed but, as far as I know, seldom shown. It gave me a valuable experience and it enabled my friend to realize the ambition of making his own film but apart from this the whole thing was not a success. Jill Owenska had her own script-writer but I think she had ambitions in this line because every day she rewrote the script and we had a moment of panic when scenes we had rehearsed and planned had to be revised.

The story was melodramatic but not unappealing. A stallion escapes from a stud-farm in the Highlands and reverts to its natural state. One does not know the breed of the stallion but as Henry looked so much a stallion with his great crest and his voice he was ideal for the part. The stud-farm is owned by an old man and one night he is beaten by intruders; the stallion comes back to attack them. Later the old man gets lost in the mountains and the stallion finds him and carries him home to safety. Then the intruders return to the house and kill the old man but at the moment the man dies the stallion senses this and returns — too late to save his master.

It was a challenge for us both. It meant having Henry loose most of the time; it also meant travelling to Scotland to find the right locations. Patricia decided this one was not for her, having never forgiven me for the Birmingham to London job, so I decided to go it alone. It was the right time of the year and the weather was good for the Highlands.

Henry and I travelled alone as Joe was involved in taking camera-crews and Jill was busy with her scriptwriters in her

chauffeur-driven Bentley. We started off in the Land-Rover and
trailer; it was a three-horse trailer so I had plenty of room for
fodder and tack. I took a sleeping-bag with me and made the
groom's section into a comfortable area for myself. I wanted to
simplify everything so that if need be I could be independent —
and I had no intention of letting the stallion out of my sight. It
was no organized trip like the second Long Ride; I went off with
no advance bookings and although Joe had hotel accommoda-
tion I was not sure at that stage whether I wanted to use it.

I enjoyed the drive up north; I had no problems and Henry
was very settled. He showed his appreciation and liked my
constant attention. It seemed he realized he was having me to
himself. Up to that time, at some part of each day, he had had
someone else attend him, and now I was determined to be the
only one. We arrived at our first location quite late. Having
travelled more slowly than the others I was the last to arrive and
Joe and Jill were keen to drag me off to meet the cast.

'Let's get this straight,' I said. 'I am not free until the stallion is
happy and settled — and this will be the rule throughout the
picture.'

They raised their eyebrows, but Henry had made a great hit
with Jill so I felt she sympathized a little.

'Well, can we meet at the hotel later?' she asked. 'It is
necessary —'

I agreed. Provided the hotel was near the stables I intended to
sleep there too — but it wasn't. 'In that case, old boy — I shall
sleep here with you,' I told Henry. I had found a good stable
and I backed the trailer up to the door where I could sleep in the
groom's section within a few yards of his box.

I did go and meet the cast of the film and we discussed our
programme. I had already read a script and knew the sequence
of shots; the first scene was in the stud-farm and there were no
problems. We had already found a stud in a beautiful setting
and I agreed to meet everyone there early the following day. I
sensed Joe's horror at my insisting I did not sleep at the hotel
but I did try and explain my motives. I don't think he
understood them very well.

Henry sensed immediately that I was staying close by. He
looked over his door every now and again and later he lay down.
I peeped in and spoke once or twice to him and he was perfectly
relaxed.

We were awake early, and long before the stable-owner arrived I had Henry watered, fed and groomed. He whinnied at the sight of the man as if warning me of his approach.

'Where are you off to today?' the man asked.

I told him and he was duly impressed. 'Nice place that,' he said. 'I remember going there when I was a youngster.'

'Is it still run as a stud?' I asked.

'Oh yes, but it's got a bit run down.'

I paid him then and soon after left for my destination. I had no difficulty finding the stud although the signs were faded and unreadable. Everyone knew of the place. I arrived on the stroke of nine by the stable clock. No-one else had appeared but the owner said he had been warned to expect the camera crew from the early hours.

'It's not like a big film unit,' I explained. 'It's only a small private set-up. I doubt if they've left their hotel yet!'

The delay gave me time to get Henry settled into a lovely big stallion box. He kept trying to see the grey mare in the box next door and as he seemed so keen I thought I ought to take a look myself. She was an unusual mare, not a bit like the others at the stud.

'How is she bred?' I asked.

'I have her here for a friend,' said the owner. 'She is a Yugoslavian Lipizzaner.'

'No!' I exclaimed, my interest very much aroused. He could tell me enough about her breeding for me to realize she was not directly related to Henry. Her name was Greyhawk. When Jill and Joe arrived I told them about the mare and said I hoped we could somehow use her in the film. Jill thought this would be possible — but of course she would have to consult her script-writers.

By ten-forty-five most of the crew had assembled and we actually completed our first shot by twelve-thirty that day. It was a simple shot showing the actor leading the stallion into the yard and then three small incidents involving others and finally mares arriving at the stud-farm. I then acted as the box-man and we had a scene with a client who inspected the stallion before leaving his mare for service. Joe enjoyed himself thoroughly that first day, and we all felt happy with the first day's shooting.

Henry showed his personality and was very amenable towards the actor, who let the stallion inspect him thoroughly. The first

126

time he led him out Henry was very saucy but I hid behind a door and warned him to behave himself — which seemed to work.

I had dinner with the unit that evening but excused myself early so that I could return to the yard and be near Henry for my second night. He knew I was approaching as soon as he heard my footsteps on the cobblestones. I heard his soft snicker as he spoke to me and he greeted me with a rub with his head. That night he woke me once by whinnying loudly from the box and Greyhawk answered — I went to him and found him staring into the yard. It was as if he had momentarily suspected I was no longer there . . .

In the days that followed I established an unprecedented closeness with Henry. He accepted this contact and showed signs that he was attuned to my thoughts. Some of the scenes required him to go free and I had no difficulty in getting him back to me. I think I became an anchor at last; and I knew I could not fail him with my commitment now. In this film I realized I needed the closeness to help his performance, in fact without it he probably could not have done what he did. It was different from the work we had done before; here it was the animal by himself and the help from me was remote.

Every day and every night I was there with him. If I got up in the night he knew it, no matter how quiet I was. If I went to get his feed he spoke to me but if I went to the same place for another purpose he merely looked with ears pricked. I felt he recognized signs — thoughts — and I learned his language of sounds. There were many sounds he made which up till then had meant little to me, but now I began to understand their meaning. If I did not actually break the barrier, at least I was allowed to glimpse the other side.

The language between animal and man is only understood by someone who has been close enough to that animal to perceive its behaviour patterns; perceiving them, and animal and man responding each in his own way towards the other, creates the language, which is not always a matter of sound, but also of signs. Let us say that anticipation and awareness of the other's purpose brings a language of attunement. Two people living together can each anticipate the thoughts of the other by an

127

unconscious recognition of signs — extrasensory perception; with an animal, if one is prepared to identify oneself, the same thing will apply. In the language of the horse towards man there are many combinations of sounds and signs that must be recognized if communication is to develop. It takes a long time to recognize this language, but no language can be learned easily and quickly, and essentially it must be one free of the emotion of fear. All animals have an instinctive suspicion of fear and no-one who is afraid can achieve the necessary closeness. People who have been brought up with animals have an advantage because they already know there is nothing to be afraid of.

I tested Henry at different times so that he did not associate the action with the routine of the day. I then waited for him to speak. At first this took the form of a snicker of the nostrils, but eventually I realized that this sign used together with another one, say a snicker with throaty overtones, meant something else. Taking the idea of language a stage further I would start a routine and then change to another. This would bring out a new, deeper throaty sound together with a blowing or vibration of the false nostril. If I went to do one thing and then 'forgot' it altogether I was amazed to see in the eye, the angle of the ears, a questioning. Only by a closeness of communion and one that is built up over a period of time can this be recognized, I think; but to me it was obvious. My friend Vera Cody has since corroborated my own findings. Asking her new mare to speak to her, she has found the horse raising her head and struggling with a new sound in the throat; perhaps we can describe this as a strangled whinny! The fact that the horse does this on command surely proves intelligence.

I was convinced that here was equine intelligence making an effort to communicate with man. Whether this intelligence was built up over centuries of domestic contact with man I do not know. Where can one find a truly wild horse today? Even when one handles a newly born foal one can feel a relaxed trust, and contact is not difficult to build up. So-called rogue situations always turn out to be due to the way man has abused this trust along the way or in the beginning. I think that with Henry I proved the trust was still there; he was lucky because he was loved from the beginning and understood. He had a lot to offer me and my discoveries were intensely thrilling. I could interpret a hundred meanings, all of them a combination of sounds, head

128

movement, ear movement, and movement of the mouth and nostrils. I discovered the language went even further — there was tail swishing and leg movement. Stallions do tend to strike with their forelegs, but Henry never did this unless he thought he had reason; a greeting for instance, or together with ear movement a warning.

Now I came the closest I had ever been to a horse and I began to realize why Vera got so much from her horses. My theory was being proved every minute of the day.

'The script says you must have the stallion free at night and he must come to a hill and look down at the farm,' said Joe. For our first night-shot we chose a wonderful place and waited for a full moon. Jill said she would find it too eerie so decided not to come. We took plenty of sandwiches and hot coffee and settled down for a long night. This was mostly spent waiting for clouds to part and then frantic action to get the shots for the scene.

Henry seemed to think it great fun and I tried him in the first rehearsal on a lunging-rein. He came to the hill and looked about him; we flashed a light and he stared at it with his ears pricked.

'That's it,' said Joe. 'Now let's do it without the rein.'

I slipped the collar from Henry's neck and told him what to do. He cantered away — Joe stopped him on the hill with a word and someone flashed the light. Henry turned slowly and stared down at it. He tossed his great mane, obliterating his eyes, and then struck out with a foreleg.

'Super!' gasped Joe, and the cameras continued to turn.

I was slowly coming up the slope — and then the stallion turned and disappeared down the other side.

'Henry!' I called, but he was gone.

The moon, having gone behind a bank of cloud, did not help. Everything in the distance disappeared into blackness. We walked about, falling into pot-holes and cursing, for nearly an hour. Then I suddenly had a thought. 'You go off home,' I said to Joe. 'Leave me here on the hill.' He argued at first but I was determined. 'If you find him at the stables then come back and tell me — if you don't, then forget me and go to bed!'

The unit packed up, got into their cars and drove off. The clouds parted and the moon came out. I stayed near the hill and when it grew cold I went and sat in the Land-Rover. I should think it was not more than fifteen minutes later when I heard a sound. I recognized it as Henry's 'Are you there?' voice and I slowly clambered out of the Land-Rover and walked back to the hill. I stood there very still and he silently came up behind me and I knew by his touch and his voice he had deliberately come back to me.

'You're a bad lad,' I said. 'Come on. We must go home.'

He loaded quietly and we drove off. Later when I settled him into his stable he tucked into his feed. And when I slipped into my sleeping-bag and called 'Good-night', he came over to his door, peered out and answered me. I was moved and lay for a long while thinking about it. Perhaps he had needed this companionship; we impose fairly artificial rules on our animals and expect them to be faithful at word of command. We forget their instinct, stronger than ours, has been blunted by civilization and we seldom make allowances for their inscrutable sensitivity.

As the film progressed I got to know the owner of the stud-farm very well. He was keen on Henry and made a point of asking his friend, the owner of Greyhawk, to come up north to see him. I discovered too that Henry was very keen on Greyhawk — in fact we had a love-affair going on in the stable-yard. The owner of the Yugoslavian Lipizzaner proved anxious to come to Scotland and I guessed he would ask to let Henry cover his mare. It did seem a heaven-sent opportunity.

Joe and Jill wanted us to travel further north for more location shots but I waylaid the proposal until after Greyhawk's owner had paid his visit. Joe was mad and said we were not just up there for fun, but I insisted and thanks to Jill I got my way.

'It'll only take a day,' she said. 'And there are two more scenes I would like to do here at the stud.'

'I thought we had finished here,' Joe argued.

'Well — I was toying with the idea of these two scenes. It would have meant calling here again on the way home . . .'

Having got my way I tactfully withdrew and went off to see Henry. He greeted me and we had a flippant conversation for a little while before I groomed him. He liked this personal contact very much and if I stopped grooming he would put his head down towards my hands, obviously asking me to continue. I have had this experience with my Alsatian who asks you to

130

continue grooming by placing a paw on your knee. Every day I had signs from the stallion telling me what he wanted from me, very much the same reactions I would get from my dog.

Greyhawk's owner turned out to be a well-known dressage rider and naturally we arranged that I would give a display for him on Henry. We made quite a thing of it and invited local people and the film unit and their friends. Greyhawk was ridden first and I was impressed by the balanced performance her owner gave. I rode the mare myself in a short dressage test and then Joe brought Henry into the ring for me.

He looked marvellous as usual and everyone cheered him spontaneously. He loved this, of course. On the spur of the moment I stood still and called him to me; Joe let him go and Henry marched over and stood at attention in front of me. 'Hullo,' I said — and much to everybody's delight, he answered me with his wonderful voice. I was glad I gave this little display because I sensed it impressed the film unit and they gave Henry more respect afterwards.

The show went like a dream. Jill found some music which she had taped and I gave an impromptu performance, deciding on movements that fitted the tune at the time; it worked very well. I made one or two errors but managed to change the routine smoothly so that it looked as if I had rehearsed and knew the sequence.

Greyhawk's owner rode Henry in the same dressage test I had used and it was like a comic turn. We were all laughing so much that in the end he had to come to a halt and retire! He was very good-natured about it and was laughing himself all the time. First I held Henry for him to mount. I thought he had got hold of the stallion (who always stood like a rock) and turned to leave him. Unfortunately he was still trying to reach the stirrup and as I walked away Henry promptly followed me. I stopped and made a grab at the bridle and hung on until the man was in the saddle.

The second incident was when he rode to the letter K, made a change of rein and Henry immediately started the Spanish Walk. The man checked him successfully and got him walking through X on the centre-line for salute. At that moment Henry did the Levade and the poor man was at a loss to know how to get the stallion to go forward again. I realized suddenly that Henry was playing him up; it took me back to those early days when Patricia and I had tried to make him listen to our aids.

131

This was a display by Henry — the man might just as well not have been there. If he had not shown such surprise he might have kidded his audience that everything was intentional, but of course he had announced he was doing the same dressage test that I had done — and this was certainly not it!

When it came to canter Henry was supposed to canter from C to A, but he gave a superb display of canter-changes at every second stride, and kept it up until he had done a complete circle of the arena. Everyone clapped madly and the more response they made the more Henry showed off. 'Behave!' I hissed. 'You're not in the bull-ring now.' But he was laughing at me and I had to admit I was laughing at him. Thus encouraged, his spontaneity knew no bounds. Was there ever a horse like my Immortal Henry?

These film days were the happiest we had ever had together. I wished Patricia could have shared them with us but if she had he would have had to divide himself again and I would not have had him so completely. Life is perverse. I knew I had proved a point to myself but I also knew that my commercial life would never permit me to give Henry the life-long dedication Vera had given to her horse. We are victims of our own creation, and I hated the thought that he and I could never be so close again. I just had the hope that this affinity would remain with us in some degree in the future.

On the last day of filming we had to do the scene where Henry came back to the farm to find his master dead. I wanted to show the stallion looking sad and mournful. I did not know how I was to do this when he had such a sense of humour but I had to try.

We set the scene up and let Henry enter the yard. The intruders fled and Henry roared and struck at them as they passed. He then had to go down a long passageway to an office at the end. He did this for me like a dog, and then he had to stand over the body of his master while the cameras came in for a close-up. We did not breathe. He lowered his head and sniffed at the actor and then he put his ears back and we got a fair shot of a dejected-looking Henry. He must have been genuinely worried by the sight of the prostrate actor, whom he had got to know as his friend. Before returning to London we all celebrated at a hotel and I surprised everyone by getting the local blacksmith to shoe Henry in his rubber shoes so that he could attend the party in person. Joe was amazed when, after we

132

had had our congratulatory drinks, I told them I was returning
to the stable with Henry and spending my last night there as
usual.

'Aren't you dying to sleep in a bed again?' they asked.

'Yes, actually I am! But after nearly three months I feel I have
a duty to stick with Henry to the end.'

And I did not regret it. He expected me to be there and I
knew that if the pattern was to be broken in London it most
certainly could not be broken there in the Highlands.

19

The End

All kinds of things happened when we returned to the London stables. Patricia had accepted a contract with a film company to use the stable-yard for scenes in the film *The Affair at the Villa Fiorita*; I was asked to go to Bristol to appear on the BBC programme *Going for a Song*; and two advertising companies needed 'lots of grey horses' for a stunt in Richmond Park. Besides this we had the offer of some property down in Sussex. 'It looks as if the property will have to wait again,' I said. 'Never mind — we'll find what we want one day . . .'

The film company descended upon us and we had to ask neighbours to help in finding space for all their equipment. There were catering marquees to go up and huge generators, to say nothing of dozens of cars and caravans. The old yard looked beautiful with hanging baskets, white doves and freshly painted stable-doors. Many years later I saw the film on television and was impressed, and nostalgic, for the yard as it was then. Out of every box there was a white head, and Henry aristocratically lorded it over them all. We had thick sound-deadening curtains draped across the archway and as the scenes were acted under lights the cobbled interior took on an air of artificiality. The American director kept telling everyone how authentic the set was and the actors seemed dutifully impressed.

While we were working on this film one of the camera-crew recognized me — and Henry. He was surprised to find us in our home setting, having seen us only on studio lots and locations. I was pleased to show him round and he was genuinely happy to discover the stallion in his own stable surrounded by his mares and ponies.

I was busy with this film for some time, which was a pity because I only saw Henry in the evenings. I hated losing the

134

contact we had built up but there was no escape and Patricia had to exercise and look after him for me. He knew she loved him as much as I did, and I think he understood the link between Patricia and myself; we had learned to ride him together and shared those early days. I think he responded to both of us with the same willingness.

One of the scenes I had to do in this film was to drive a Land-Rover and trailer down the narrow high street of Sunbury-on-Thames and into a tiny forecourt of a house. Getting in was easy but reversing out practically impossible. I had to reverse into the busy little street, reverse a quarter of a mile down it, and then position myself for another take. This went on all day with police help, and I got hotter under the collar every minute. I had a line to say in the scene and I said something different each time. The continuity-girl asked me what I was going to say and I agreed the phrase only to add another variation the next time I said it. The director kept telling everybody that not only was the stable-yard authentic but I was 'for real' too.

The picture ended, and then we solved the other problems as well. I was late getting to Bristol for my programme but, having guessed the nearest values of some antique clocks, came home with a lovely prize.

The Richmond Park scene was not very easy and after some hilarious moments I decided it would be best done in a field. Finding the right location with park-like background proved difficult but we did eventually find what we wanted in Surrey.

'I want them all to gallop across the sky-line —' drawled the man in charge — 'and then I want them to stop, rear up and be seen in silhouette against the setting sun.'

'All right,' I answered.

We got the first take with the horses galloping across the sky-line but the second was much more difficult. However, after a lot of persuasion we were able to get four of them to stop in full flight and rear up in front of the cameras. 'Oh,' said the young camera-man. 'We weren't ready — could we do that again?' 'You must be joking,' I gasped, but he wasn't — so we galloped them off again and made them stampede into rearing on the same spot. We got the same four horses and then everyone thought they had the shots they required. 'Good,' I said. 'Now let's catch the horses and go home.'

135

Most of them came easily to feed-buckets but Henry's friend Merrylegs decided she would rather stay behind. It was getting dark and my helpers were not too keen to stay. 'She must want to come now we have loaded the others,' I said. 'What on earth's got into her!'

Eventually she gave in — smilingly, of course! Perhaps she felt she had an affinity with the surroundings; a lovely green field is very tempting to a pony, especially one that has lived in London for some time. 'Never mind,' I promised. 'We will find our farm soon — then you can live more as nature intended!'

Patricia had several farms lined up for us to see and we intended to visit them as soon as things settled down. We did go and see one or two but they either needed too much money spent on them or they were miles from any decent riding country. But then something happened at home that caused us some worry — Henry went lame on his off-hind.

'It's the leg which has the scar,' said Patricia. 'His old bull-fighting wound.'

The vet thought he might have a strain or even rheumatism. We treated and hosed the leg for ages every day and rode him in bandages. It did get better but every now and again the stallion would show momentary signs of lameness.

'Ride him without shoes,' said the blacksmith. 'He has very hard boxy feet, it should do him good.'

We did this for about three months. Henry went very well without shoes and the blacksmith thought his feet had improved. He showed occasional signs of lameness but it never seemed to worry him. I suppose he could have been ridden without shoes from then on but I was stupid enough to think he would be better shod. Now I realize that once the feet harden and the going is fair, and provided the horse is an even mover, shoes are not a necessity. However, we had him re-shod — and then the awful thing happened.

Henry had acclimatized himself to being unshod, and the first night he had shoes on again he must have slipped through the thick bedding onto the cobbled floor — or perhaps he slipped getting up. The next morning we found he had an enormous rupture.

The vet said there was nothing he could do and the poor old horse went lame again. I exercised him at liberty in the school and he would dance about oblivious of his condition. It took him a week to get used to the rupture and then his mind took over and he was like his normal self again; he would tease me in the school, chase me and follow me doing the Spanish Walk. But I knew I would never ride him again.

'We must get our farm now,' I said. 'We must get Henry and the mares away from here. Surely we can find the country home for them, if we try . . .

House-hunting took precedence from then on. We searched the whole of Sussex and found one or two places which seemed suitable. One was on the South Downs and the other in Ashdown Forest. 'Henry should be got away now!' advised the vet. But we could not get our affairs sorted out as quickly as that. The old yard in London had to be sold or have a manager and the new place would have to be re-fenced for the grey mares and have built stallion-boxes and a covered school.

Then we met an old friend in Sussex who had just moved to a wonderful stud-farm. It had everything: double-fenced pad-docks, stallion-boxes, foaling-boxes and a hundred acres bord-ered by forest.

'Let us have Henry here until you find what you want,' said the friend. She had always loved him and thought the world of him. It seemed a good idea and we presumed it would only be for a short time. Decisions have to be made in life and our paths are chosen by them; if Henry had not been the right one at the time to go into the bull-ring he would not have had his injury and without this he would not have gone lame when he did. If I had not had him re-shod he would not have ruptured himself . . . The decisions from now on had to be mine. We thought the stud-farm was the kindest decision for him and so we agreed to take him there.

I travelled with him in the box. He sweated a lot but was pleased to have my company; I knew because he kept rubbing his head on my chest. It was a precious moment; once again I was his anchor and the barriers were down. I stood in the box all the way to the farm. We stopped once at an inn and had a ploughman's lunch and lots of people came out to admire Henry. It was like old times — he was still the same, he loved the attention and used his voice and tossed his mane. We had trodden a long road together, he and I, full of glamour and adventure, and I hoped it would continue for some time to come.

137

The stud-farm was beautifully secluded and set in a valley full of small hills and sheltered paddocks. It was strange that the forest rising up on two sides made it like a miniature corner of Austria, like the stud-farm where Henry had been born. Our friend came to greet us and showed enormous pleasure in giving our little stallion a home. I offered to pay for his keep but she let me know in no uncertain terms that having Henry there was all the reward she could want. This was the effect he had on everybody.

As our friend had only just moved to the farm she had very little stock and most of this was kept in. 'If you think he would like to go into a paddock during the day there is a double-fenced paddock adjoining the main yard,' she said. I thought this was a wonderful idea, knowing how Henry would love to feel free in a grassy meadow.

We unloaded him and walked him into the main yard. He inspected his large airy box. 'Bigger than the box you had in London,' I told him. He snorted and sniffed at the deep-litter bed, examined the automatic water-bowl suspiciously and made a funny face at the feed manger. I was reminded that Vera Cody only had to say to Goldie: 'Make a funny face!' and he would immediately put his head in the air and raise his upper lip! 'You're being silly, Henry,' I said. 'Come on — you're going out to grass.'

We led him on a rope-halter and on the spur of the moment I gave Patricia a leg-up onto his back. She was the last person to ride him.

We took him into the paddock and I let him free. All three of us stood watching as he cantered away to a small hill, where he gazed out across the pine trees, his head up, ears pricked and his mane stirred by a breeze ... I called him back to me and he came and I rubbed his neck with my hand. 'I'll be back very soon, old boy — and we'll have our own farm,' I whispered. He was happy. He cantered away and stood on the little hill, snatched a mouthful of grass and gazed again at the forest. This is the picture I shall always want to remember. It is the picture I shall never forget.

One week later our friend telephoned in tears. Henry had fallen into a ditch and broken a blood-vessel, and before the vet could get to him he had died.

We were all heart-broken. But although I blamed myself over and over again, no-one was really to blame for his death. If we had made different decisions things could have been better — or worse. Who can know what fate has in store?

All stories must have an end — but I am not sure that the end is always death. Perhaps after all the end is the beginning. I have always believed that the pattern of life is to be born again, not necessarily in the same form as before, but that we all belong to an eternal spirit that gives life continuously. Nature, after all, rejuvenates itself over and over again. I could end my story like a fairy-tale and say everyone lived happily ever after. Is this what they meant in the ancient tales — we go on happily ever after, like the tree of life which renews itself every spring?

We found our farm and we took our grey mares away from London. When I looked out of my window and saw them in the paddocks framed by the South Downs I dreamed of Henry who had not come with us. How I wished he had.

Months went by, and then I telephoned the stud in the Highlands. For I had let Henry serve the Yugoslavian mare. How thrilled we all were to discover that Greyhawk had a colt foal at foot!

Postscript

I am sitting in the conservatory with huge Coleus, Bougainvillaea, Red Peppers and Geraniums, which Patricia grows with her green fingers, and I can see into the South Meadow where the horses graze. In a way Henry is still with us . . .

Greyhawk eventually came to live with us and the foal grew into a beautiful but temperamental brown colt. Reluctantly we decided to have him cut but before this we bought a lovely grey mare for ourselves which we called Henrietta. We fell for this mare because she had a 'Henry' look about her, the long mane, the proud bearing and an educated ride. It was a sudden and nostalgic impulse that made us give her the name we did. It was also around this time we bought our stud-farm at last and the brown colt, while all the grey horses were removed from London, was reprieved. Horaya, the Arabian stallion, sired a grey colt foal, and before the brown was finally cut he served Henrietta and she had a very pretty grey filly, whom we called Ella.

As I look out of the window at this moment I can see Henry's granddaughter, Horaya's son, and my lovely old Henrietta. Two months ago Greyhawk died. Unfortunately grey horses are often subject to cancerous growths under the tail which get larger as they grow older. Greyhawk had them and the vet thought they would start to grow internally. She had a stoppage which he could not reach and by the next morning she was dead. I found her sitting up with her head resting against the bars of the big isolation box. She looked as if she had suffered a bit, her big eyes were open and her long mane curled over her face. She had lived to a riper age than Henry, whose exact age we had never known for certain but whom we thought of as about fifteen when he died.

140

I feel nothing for dead bodies. To me the person or animal is no longer there; I don't need a grave to mourn over. The flesh returns to the earth and the spirit joins the eternity that is still going on around us. With this philosophy there is no real end to anything, only immortality.

If I stand in the silence of the evening and look at the horses in the field I can feel a closeness that is forever. If I walk in the meadow with my dogs and Henrietta comes to speak to me I believe she comes because she wants to come. Does she know I bought her when my need was greatest; did she sense we called her Henrietta as a token to our past love? I must believe all this because if I do then I can sense that she believes it too. We do not reach an understanding in our solitude without believing what we need to know.

Horaya's son had burrs in his tail and when I went to take them out he stood still for me. I said nothing while I unravelled his tail and he raised his hind foot. I gave no response and he did it again. The next time he lifted the foot and pushed it out towards me. 'Don't you dare!' I said, and when he got the reaction he wanted he didn't try it again. I have to smile at him, he is so like his dad.

Henry's granddaughter is a kind mare with none of her grandfather's fire but some of his spirit. She shows natural rhythm but needs strong handling, otherwise she loses her collection. She has a majestic reluctance to drink from her stable bucket, and whenever you pass her door with a bucket of water she asks for a drink; we have to hold the heavy bucket up to her and she usually swallows the lot! In this strange habit she is more royal than royalty itself, for her grandfather was always content to drink from his bucket on the stable floor.

It is old Henrietta who steals our hearts; there is such a strong something in the way she looks at you and talks to you. When Henry had gone she took over the ponies Magic and Merry and guarded them with her life. In the fields she would not allow the other horses near them, and it was very touching to see the small ponies sheltering next to her and using her tail to flick the flies from their faces. Both the ponies have now gone.

The last job Henrietta did for me in London was the film tests for *The Charge of the Light Brigade.* She was ridden by David Hemmings and Corin Redgrave and I gave the director, Tony Richardson, a riding lesson on the mare after each session. I still have the empty champagne bottles they used to open and drink at the start of each day's shooting.

In the South Meadow there are other grey horses — I cannot have any other colour now, in memory of Henry. The photographers from London have been down this year to take new shots of the horses in their country home. No doubt I shall be finding more Christmas and birthday cards in the shops with my grey horses on them; there will be pictures of Henry's granddaughter and of Horaya's son to remind us of the other cards we collected years ago.

When the horses are out at grass and we call them in they come immediately. Each one knows his or her own box in the yard, they never make a mistake, and if I change them it takes only a day for them to know their new boxes. I often used to watch people in the London stables putting horses away, and would offer advice and instruction. Down here people need to do nothing, the horses actually put themselves away. Because horses react slowly some people dismiss them as unintelligent, but if you wait for their reaction the results are always positive.

The weather is getting wintry and soon we shall be bringing the horses in at night. When it rains and the wind blows cold in September I start to worry in the night, and eventually I break under the strain and have them brought in. Then when the weather is bad I am smug with the thought that they are in their boxes, rugged up, with bulging haynets and the owls for company. I can then look from my bedroom window across the home paddock to the stable-yard shadowed in trees, perhaps a moon making the flint barn white and the field beyond shrouded in mist. If I walk over and creep silently into the yard for a moment I can hear the contented munch of hay, but as a twig snaps under my feet one head after another will look out and I am greeted by the soft snicker of nostrils. One or two will lick my hand, while others will turn back to their hay. I think Henrietta senses something because she will stand with me longer than the others.

Dear mare . . . I am sure she would have loved him too . . .